The successful coach

The choice is yours, Maxi!

Marijan Hizak

Keep on keeping on

All greatness

C'mon The Town .

Translated by Sandra Hizak
Edited by Peter Hopwood
Cover illustration by Tiva Tiskara

To all of those whose bags are always ready...

Contents

20. Speaking and listening as indispensable tools

21. Say, point and include the players

22. The power of positive thinking

23. Self-confidence can be crucial in swaying the odds

24. Always fair play

25. Every crisis means an opportunity

26. The football managerial merry-go-round

27. What do people think of you?

28. The person I am

29. The crucial role of a coach in conflict situations

30. Do not justify defeat

31. The greatness of a coach shines through in tough times

32. No success without parental cooperation and support

33. Is quality essential in determining the price of a coach?

34. Knowledge is vital for success

35. Becoming a brand increases competitiveness

36. Do coaches earn too much?

37. Use every free moment to relax

38. The majority fail to understand why you're attacked

39. Coaches need to mature

40. Is polite behaviour a sign of weakness?

41. Reacting to public criticism

42. Never regard sports journalists as enemies

43. Coaches on the rise or fall - never refuse journalists

68. Start thinking positively and you'll see how your life changes

69. The coaching profession of tomorrow

70. Greatness is attainable

A word from the author

For me, this book is magical, just like Ireland - the country where it was written. Why do I feel it's magic? Simply because after you've finished reading, you'll see magical things start to happen. It will open the way to personal sporting achievements, coaching success and spiritual wealth. Just in the same way, moving to Ireland has brought me and my family magical peace, happiness and immense joy. The topics covered in this book have never before been published in this form and I'm confident this will become an indispensable daily handbook for coaches and athletes, as well as those in business who work with and manage teams. When you start applying the philosophy found in the pages of this book, get ready for positive life changes. Not only will these changes ease your daily challenges and tension, but equally, they will also prepare you for success in your own field. So, how was this book put together? As a former football player and marketing executive at the professional football club *NK Varteks* in Croatia, I spent a large part of my career alongside sports coaches, following their success. In my time I've had numerous meetings, been involved with so many sports matches, travelled far and wide and spent hours and hours discussing football and the coaching profession with football coaches.

Today I'm grateful to them for that, because I'm one of the privileged who had the opportunity and blessing to be able to hear and take on board so much great educational and experience-based knowledge from these coaches. And not just any coaches I might add – those from the top level! Notably, one who was in fact the head of the Croatian national football team which won 3rd place at the 1998 FIFA World Cup Finals in France. I could never have dreamt that one day, this coaching knowledge that I seemed to absorb like a sponge for all those years, and diligently writing notes, would bring permanent discomfort, both professional and intimate. I only eventually managed to suppress these feelings when I moved from Croatia to Ireland. Thanks to the support and encouragement of a certain great football supporter, but above all a great man, named Mark Kavanagh, known locally as Maxi, was I able to transform my know-how and turn it into the book you now hold in your hands. To make it even more interesting to readers, within the stories there's a part of my own life story. I share my own life's low points and successes which are interweaved with the glorious achievements of my three sons Filip, Jakov and Juraj. This is my third book but it's my first Irish book. It's Irish in every way. It was written in Ireland thanks to the encouragement of a great Irish man, thanks to my wife, who translated the original Croatian text into English in

Ireland, thanks to Peter Hopwood, an avid football connoisseur who proofread the text and thanks to my Irish friend Richard. Of course, the pulse of the book takes place in the cult Irish Stadium, Oriel Park in Dundalk. It's simple. If you want to become a successful leader and team player, (and not just in Ireland), apply the philosophy of this book, and see the changes take place. The choice is yours!

1. The defeat that unlocked my door of greatness

Oriel Park has been empty for quite a while now. There's not a living soul to be found. The thunderous roar of the crowd was replaced by the bitterness of defeat, which now floats like dew over the nearby bars and pubs where conversations of the home team are shared while sipping a pint of Guinness. Apart from my office, the only light was coming from the room of the kit man, Yuri. When it was time to leave, taking the stairs leading to the exit, I couldn't avoid his door. Every time we met, he gave me a warm welcome. We would sometimes exchange a few words about the quality of the sports equipment, but never anything personal about the players or the way my team had played. With the recent crushing defeat of my team firmly on my mind, today as I bumped into Yuri, I skipped my conventional "Hi, how are you?" and I asked him what he thought of the match. In a low and calm voice he replied: "Maxi, I can't comment because I didn't watch the match." The answer surprised me, but I accepted it silently. The next day, after training, I used the opportunity to find out a little more about our kit man. I wondered how it was possible that someone who spends every day at the stadium among the players, didn't watch such a significant game? Yuri, as he was affectionately known to the players by his Russian name, was not, in fact, Russian at all. His real name was Juraj (George). I was quite surprised when I discovered that Yuri was no less than one of the best Croatian players in the mid-seventies, and in 1994 voted the best young Croatian coach. After I learned this, I was intrigued to know what had become of him, not knowing that he would soon become my mentor, and in a very short time change my coaching principles from the ground up. Over time we met on many occasions and during this time I won three best coach in Ireland awards and five prestigious league titles. On Friday after training I deliberately lingered a little longer in his office, which gave me a chance to talk with Yuri at length. I invited him for a drink in a nearby pub. He didn't take up my offer but instead, warmly invited me to have a cup of tea with him at his place. We chatted about this and that. Yuri didn't hold back when talking about his bitter fate that had followed him throughout his life. He spoke of his glorified positive attitude and thoughts that allowed him to be present every day looking forward to going to work and enjoying the most beautiful sport in the world - football. Yuri's coaching career was abruptly short lived by alcohol addiction. Having lost everything in life - his wife, his home and all of his money, he went to a Christian community retreat in the hope that staying there would help wipe away this vicious addiction. He succeeded. The Cenacolo Community brought back his faith in life. He stayed in their homes in Medjugorje and Saluzzo, ending up in Ireland, in their home in Knock, Co. Mayo. Thanks to the kindness of the brothers of St. Dominic, after one year in Knock he made his way to Dundalk, taking up a job at a local football club as a kit man. Due to his humility and respectfulness, he soon became the most popular person at the club. I began spending more and more time with Yuri. We delved into various topics which developed into full discussion. Today, it's simply unthinkable for me to leave the stadium without having a cup of tea with Yuri. Why so unthinkable? You'll no doubt see for yourself when you've read this book. The fruit of my friendship with Yuri over tea, has become a collection of 70 stories which I wrote down and truly unlocked the door of my greatness. I'm sure they'll unlock yours too!

2. The successful coach who "digs the most gold"

A football coach is nothing more than a manager in a gold mine. Don't misunderstand me, Maxi - gold in this metaphor represents the players. A successful coach is one who digs the most gold, which always has to be of high quality to meet the demands of the media, the public, the sporting public and sponsors. To achieve this, it's simply not enough to be just a 'leader" of the miners. He must be a visionary. A strategist. Someone who will determine the ways and means to bring the miners to the "gold". Maybe you'll find my comparison with a gold mine ridiculous? After extensively following Irish and Croatian coaches, this gives me every right to say that this is correct.

The strongest confirmation of this claim of mine is backed up by watching the paths of football players who have reached their peak under the leadership of Croatian coaches such as Miroslav Blazevic and Branko Ivankovic. These players today represent the future of Croatian football. Players such as Kranjcar, Suker, Boban, Modric, Mandzukic, and Kovacic represent a mere fraction of the great players whose careers were led by Blazevic and Ivankovic. In carrying out the coaching, the "mining work", a lot of coaches have been helped by the fact they are thorough and meticulous, studious and professional. This is why it's extremely important that the coach is a team player. To be clear, the team must always know who has the final word. The coach must, after taking over the team, establish quality two-way communication with his colleagues and players. He must present his vision of achieving the set goals so the members of his team can easily put it into practice. Maxi, never underestimate your status. You're the leader of the team. You're the moving spirit. Your role is the most important in terms of synergy. Football is not a fool's game as some may think. Football is a mind game, where it's just not enough to run fast but also be a quick thinker. The heart of the tactics set by the coach is the off-the-ball movement, the speed of receiving the ball, open play etc. When working with players, apart from the technique, tactics and physical conditioning, as a coach you have to take into account the psychological, social and cultural environment of the team. You need to trust your players and associates by actively involving them in your work. Sadly, the sporting public doesn't value "coach miners" enough. Today the sport is dominated exclusively by the desire for successful results. You've either got it - or you haven't. If you've got it, you're successful. If you haven't, then it's time to pack your bags. I think the competition result by no means should be the only measurement of the quality of a coach's work.

True coaches should be valued according to the "gold" they dig!

3. More than a game of 11-a-side

The game of football is often unjustifiably and sarcastically referred to as "a simple game for the masses". The truth is completely different. Football is much more than a simple game of 11-a-side. There's no other team sport where the individual quality of a player is as significant as in football. Playing with only your legs, the speed of play and the constant change from defence to attack and vice-versa, guarantees the unpredictability of the game. In football only set-play from corners, free-kicks and penalties are predictable. Not without reason, football today has become "the most interesting irrelevant issue in the world". Football is, above all, a mind game. A game that makes high demands of players and coaches, demands that are not easy to respond to. Football players, in addition to mastering techniques for manipulating the ball with their feet and physical qualities, must have intelligence for the game and an ability to understand it at any point. Maxi, only amateurs think it's easy to choose the best solution for the team from the wide variety of options available to them. Also, not everyone can simply be a football coach. In order to become a successful coach it's no longer enough to bring together players who want to play, who can control the ball and who are in great physical condition. In order to take productive quality steps forward in football, a perception of time, space and situation is needed. Maxi, you have a reputation as a coach who is great at "reading the game". This can only mean one thing - that you're extremely knowledgeable in football and intellectually powerful. Only intellectually capable individuals are able to anticipate the reactions of rivals, and to "read their game". The same is true for the players as their intellectual capacity is just as important as controlling the ball and physical fitness. Someone quite rightly compared football to geometry. Opening and closing spaces on the pitch are logical mathematical motions. Football is an art of unpredictability. Very little can be predicted in football. There's always natural spontaneity meaning one wrong move, a miscalculation from the referee or just one touch of the ball can change everything - eagerly awaited by twenty-two players. The coach not only follows and anticipates what happens in play but equally detects and corrects errors on the pitch at the right time, especially tactically; how to set up the game and the right time to send on a sub and make a change.

4. Set goals are an expression of a common pursuit

It's a kind of art form to build a successful team in sport. Not even the greatest coaches in the world succeed overnight. No, Maxi, I'm not exaggerating when describing the process of creating a team. I know, it's not a coach's game, but it is a player's game. Although it's the players who are physically playing, the coach is the one who holds a clear vision of the game and the team, and transforms it into practice with the players. The coach must help players to fully understand what it means to be a team. He needs to encourage players to realize the team's common success is a multiplied result of their individual successes. When they're encouraged in this way, when players feel that they're better than the other team, this can only be recognized and rewarded. It takes time to form "the team". It's a painstaking process of creation and sacrifice. When you manage to make the players support one another, you've already completed most of the work, as the process can only continue to build and spread positively. A successful coach thinks highly of his players, recognizes and respects their individuality, including the personality of players and equally their private lives. Players should always be spoken to as equals on all issues. Players simply need to feel that they're important. When you speak to them, you need to point out their tasks and their specific roles as well as your expectations. The set goals of a team should be perceived by players as an expression of a common pursuit. The most fundamental aspect players need to understand is that the team always wins, not the individual. Individual success within a team is to be welcomed, but it's more important what the entire team is going to do. When you're accepted by the players, when they are convinced of your honesty and fairness, their anger, caused by a substitution on the pitch or not being picked for the starting eleven, disappears. Pay attention to what players under a successful coach point out in their interviews or statements: "I'm just one link in the chain." "I would never have succeeded if my play hadn't been supported by my team mates".

5. Meeting certain requirements to create offensive play

The career of every coach is always marked with a certain style of play. Certain coaches are recognized for their defensive tactics, and others, like you Maxi here in Ireland, are recognized by their attacking style of play. Your offensive profile is highlighted by the number of goals scored by the teams you've managed. The defence and attack as fundamental elements of the game are interconnected and dependent on each other. These cannot be easily trained. In my opinion, the defensive style of play is easier to grasp and adopt compared to the attack.

The creation and adoption of an offensive game requires more effort and time, but equally coaching experience. Certain requirements must be met, such as the quality set up and a player's off-the-ball movement in order to create a surplus in the game. Discipline and control is not enough. Players need to think quickly, who can rapidly open play, and swiftly get rid of the ball. Offensive football requires creativity, ideas or a touch of flamboyancy in the game. Forming an offensive game is a process that takes time both for coaches and players. To start the process, it's essential players believe and follow the coach's philosophy. The offensive style of play needs months to develop. Maxi, for the last six months you've been working on developing the adoption of the offensive concept, and still you're not pleased with the results.

Why do I acutely emphasize the importance of knowledge, expertise and experience in the process of creating play? Because for the game to function, either defensively or offensively, players and coaches need to understand such a concept, and for a coach lacking experience, who has just started his coaching career, regardless of whether he was once a top player, this poses a real challenge. Once the offensive game is formed, it represents your "ace up your sleeve". Therefore, I can't explain in words how happy you'll be when our *Lilywhites* reach the point of adopting "the desired game." We'll see Oriel Park constantly crowded, fans in ecstasy, a strong positive atmosphere within the town and around the club. The players will feel great and you'll be feeling calm and serene.

6. Half-time communication?

A break during half-time is a significant moment for the coach. It's an opportunity to draw attention to both the good, but also the negative aspects of the game. Since my kit room is just next- door to the opponent's changing room, over the last twenty years I've heard hundreds of stories and different approaches to the players at half-time. I wonder whether it's even possible in such a short time to show players everything that a coach noticed during the first half. So, what exactly is the most effective thing to do for players during a quick fifteen-minute break? To ensure the coach's messages are useful and effective, first of all they need to be short, simple and clear. Brevity and concise information is essential as there's very little time available. Players still need an additional few minutes to freshen up, rest their feet and re-energize ready to get back on the pitch. The coach's short comments during half-time should initially provide feedback to the players on their game, and instruct them how to resolve problems that have arisen in the game. This can't be done using general phrases, such as "you have to score a goal", "you're not concentrating enough" or "the defence is open." Given the short timeframe, he should concentrate on practical advice, in order to give players valuable suggestions to improve. Practical advice can often be connected to the pitch conditions, and can for example, in harsh weather conditions, subtly, and sometimes even drastically, affect the result of a game. If it rains, the surface is slippery and the ball travels faster. Do all players wear suitable boots for such conditions on the pitch? Is it windy? The team that attacks with the wind behind them certainly has an advantage over a team that plays against the wind. What's the pitch like? Is it short, long, narrow or wide? These are all factors that influence the approach of a certain game and which every coach needs to make his players aware of. Narrow pitches allow pressure inside the penalty area, therefore the defensive players should be warned when the ball is on the bounce. Players should be encouraged to constantly put pressure on the ball as it increases the possibility of an opponent's errors, and in turn increases the chances of gaining higher ball possession. Do players follow the ball and attack opponents as soon as they receive the ball, or wait? Finally, it's always useful to remind players to communicate and talk more with each other. Football is a game where you don't use your hands. But, remember - there aren't any rules prohibiting the use of your voice! Players should be encouraged to use their voices as a resource on the pitch, because communication between the players is an essential tool in defence and attack. "Watch your back!" "One-two!" "Mine!" or "I've got it covered!". During half-time it's not good to only analyse mistakes. It's also very important to emphasise the positives in the game and boost the players' motivation levels. This is something many coaches fail to do. Criticism during half-time is mostly counter-productive, especially when you are losing. A positive approach to communication enhances the confidence of players and increases the likelihood their trained skills will be repeated. The half-time break is the perfect opportunity to emphasise the goals set by the coach. Regardless of how many things the coach has on his mind, he shouldn't talk about everything. He should selectively identify a few key changes that can help improve the game in the second half. Every wise coach will always leave a little time for his players to speak during the break. Players too have a certain perspective on the game, despite the attitude of the coach. Their comments and suggestions can often be useful in addition to the coach's words during the break. Then there are the substitutions. Your predecessor Stephen Kenny was a great master of the substitution. Charismatic Stephen has a feeling for the right time to bring on subs during a match, and the interesting thing is he always uses all three changes. Substitutions are a result of how well you read the game as a coach. The course of the game simply cannot be predicted prior to the start of the game.

7. The best system does not exist

Which system of play is the best? As long as there's football Maxi, there'll always be debates on the best system of play. Along with football development, throughout history certain formations were created which determined each player's position on the pitch. This is at the discretion of the coach on a specified schedule and tasks. The system selected by the coach generally should be adapted to the team so the capacity and quality of his available players is fully optimized. The best system does not exist. The best one is the one that wins. The one optimally adapted to the physical and technical abilities of players that are available to the coach. As a young and ambitious coach, I once experimented. I tried to play each of the three basic systems: 3-5-2, 4-4-2 and 4-3-3, respecting their possible variations relating to the defence, midfield and attack. What do I think about them? Each of these systems has its own quality, but also its disadvantages.

The national teams of Germany, Brazil and Italy have all been marked in different periods by the 3-5-2 system. The historical bronze gained by my Croatian national team at the 1998 World Cup in France, led by Miroslav Blazevic also consisted of a 3-5-2 formation. Under this system, wingers are more forwardly orientated and the midfielders are used mainly to stop the possible opponents' counterattacks. Today's football is dominated by a 4-4-2 formation and its variants. I wouldn't be wrong if I said 80 percent of top clubs and national teams play with four players at the back. It's used to maintain possession of the ball and tactical control in midfield. Depending on the technical and physical abilities of the two wide midfielders, this formation is easily transformed to 4-3-3 or 4-5-1. The system is successfully used by Real Madrid and Bayern Munich, and it was particularly impressive to see how the system worked perfectly within the Spanish national team during the World Cup in 2010. Each system requires training time and needs to be automatic. It's not as simple as it seems. The system used by a successful team must be flexible and ready to implement against any opponent. Especially in today's football, in the 21st century, when football has become a game of modern technical advantages, fast, irrepressible and ruthless. With rapid defensive closures and even faster counterattacks, it's an open game. The beauty and the speed of the game have changed over time. The game itself has dramatically speeded up! When I look at footage from the last century, it seems to me the players are walking, not running. A coach who doesn't understand this, who doesn't change and fails to continuously educate himself is doomed to failure. A new time has come. Only those who follow the evolution survive. A large number of renowned coaches think that classic systems are dying out. More and more attention is now placed on the compactness and shape of the team. Preferably, the lines are flowing, and are complemented to the maximum. Unlike clubs, where the game system selection is based on the availability and quality of players, national team coaches have a pre-established legacy and well established national system of play, having to choose players according to it. Give or take, it's common for an U-21 national team to play in the system used by the senior team. Interestingly, it's the opposite for the World and European champions, as Spain's senior team usually adopts the system of the U-21 team.

8. Analysis kicks off the working week

The working week of a coach usually begins with a meeting with colleagues before the first training session after the game. This is primarily about performing the analysis of the previous match. Only after that can a meeting with the players be held. Analysis of the game should never be too long nor too varied, and has to have a dual character - psychological and technical-tactical. The psychological approach to the players mainly depends on the outcome of the last match. After defeat the coach must strive to raise the morale of the team as a whole and individuals. Following victory the coach must "keep the team firmly on the ground", and not allow players to be affected by the euphoria. During the analysis, none of the players should be individually named, criticised or publicly blamed for the defeat or negative play. These can be possibly presented to each individual player face to face in private. I once knew a coach who would never criticise players after a defeat, but instead only after a victory. Also, he never criticised the subs or younger players. He had a positive attitude towards them, encouraging their qualities. He told me that he discovered such an approach proved to be successful. When I think about it Maxi, it seems to me that his approach makes perfect sense. Do you know, Maxi, I've always found analysis after a victory to be harder. Why? Because euphoria after a victory, heavily influenced by the fans and the environment created by the players, always results in poor play or defeat in the next match. As for technical and tactical analysis, based on statistical data prepared by your assistants, you're obliged to point out the flaws during the game, but also to point out their good side, publicly giving praise to individuals for following your instructions during the game.

After defeat, as a coach you always need to be accountable in the eyes of the public. Never look for an excuse for failure, either personal or on behalf of the players. The coach is always responsible for choosing the optimal playing system, the team selection, the organization and training load. Such an approach is appreciated and respected among players. After the analysis of the match is complete, you and your expert team begin to prepare for the next match. Players have to become familiar with the plan and schedule for the current week, gradually getting to know their next opponent and the way they play. And so the first training session of the new working week begins together with the process of psychological and motivational preparation of the team for the upcoming match.

9. Are coaches always right?

Most coaches want to be right all the time. So I was pleasantly surprised when I read that if a man is right 55 percent of the time, he can be considered as great man. If you want to convince your players that certain training exercises can be done better, you should never say "I'll prove to you that this can be done better"! This is the same as telling them "You'd better listen to me, because I'm smarter than you". Defiance and conflict among players and a toxic atmosphere in the dressing room is created by these words. Players should be taught without even noticing. You also have to be careful when you persuade the media about something you're not one hundred percent sure of. You'll never embarrass yourself if you honestly admit that you may be wrong. And if you're sure your interlocutor is wrong, don't give him a rough time. You won't achieve anything at all.

A few years ago, former coach of Varteks, Zlatko Dalic, was with his then club, Al-Tain FC, in a friendly match during a break in Turkey. In the fiftieth minute he replaced Ismail Ahmed with the young player Mohanad Salem in the belief that his quality would accelerate the flow of the ball. It didn't happen. They lost the match. Following the match, during an interview, one of the journalists blamed him for the defeat. Coach Zlatko Dalic didn't like it, and tried to justify his move to the journalist. The next day during a regular scheduled press conference, the Croatian coach knew he'd be asked the same question by certain journalists. He decided to change his attitude. When the question about the substitution arose, he refrained from justifying himself, and humbly replied "To be honest, I can see now that I was wrong. I'm sorry I made this substitution". Miraculously nobody asked any more questions about the substitution, nor was it mentioned in the media ever again. So, we all can learn throughout our lives. Zlatko Dalic learned that if you want people to conform to your way of thinking, you must respect the opinion of others.

10. Coaches make mistakes, don't they?

Mistakes are an inevitable part of life. If you make mistakes, it means you're active and alive. Mistakes should be accepted as part of life. Mistakes should be always turned to our advantage, and we shouldn't blame others for them. If you did something wrong, you should think about it deeply and analyse what went wrong. Why did this mistake happen to me? Did I act without thinking? Did I hesitate too long and lose sight of exactly what I was doing? Was I distracted and in turn did something stupid? The most important aspect of all this is to recognize and admit your mistakes and then to do everything it takes not to repeat them. As a coach, difficulties arise that are simply part of the job. A coach can either solve or suppress them. What does it mean to suppress them? Maxi, this means that mistakes are distorted, denied, and shown in an opposite way from what they truly are, moved into an easier context. We like to philosophise and theorise about mistakes. All of us sometimes like to bluff others into believing in our success and strength when, in fact, the most difficult thing for us is to solve problems. The most primitive form of suppression is denial. Problems should never be transferred from difficult to easy opponents or from tricky away fixtures to comfortable home fixtures in the belief that better results will be achieved against a weaker opposition, or at home. Some coaches blame their players for failure! Pointing the finger at players is the worst move a coach can make. This is only a short-term solution. Problems mustn't be suppressed or left to someone else to solve them instead. We need to roll up our sleeves and get to work. Problems won't be miraculously solved by themselves. We're the only ones to solve them. And yes, mistakes can be a great teacher and fertile ground for personal development – as I was assured by our mutual friend, amateur coach John Malone. Although not a professional, he has a very conscientious and meticulous approach to coaching. Each time he came to a new club or before the start of the season, he would carefully outline specific goals. The process of achieving these goals was to split them into certain timeframes or stages, so- called milestones. After the completion of each stage, such as the preparation cycle, at certain parts of the season he made a brief analysis, carefully comparing the results achieved to the targeted objectives. As he had a habit of re-reading his notes from time to time, he noticed that certain errors were constantly being repeated, so he began to correct them. He also noticed, based on his notes, that the same players would always get yellow or red cards, and the same ones would, sure enough, always rebel and so on. To analyse everything, according to him, was not an easy task, but thanks to his additional education and discussion with older colleagues, he managed to keep his mistakes, including mistakes in his relationships with his players to a minimum. Today he's a successful and highly-sought-after amateur coach, primarily due to the "significant" correction of his own mistakes.

11. The overlooked benefit of an experienced coach

Maxi, your compatriot, the famous Irish writer Oscar Wilde, has an expression with a wonderful thought: "Experience is one thing you can't get for nothing." Today, how much is the experience of a coach appreciated? In the coaching profession, experience has a priceless value. Supporting this, as the late Croatian coach Djalma Markovic used to say, is "there is no difference between knowledge and the truth". Ivan Djalma Markovic was a football coach but also a philosopher. A coach who often used metaphors in communication with his players such as "don't make a phone call before you pass the ball". Ivan Djalma Markovic possessed the brilliant gift of turning complicated processes into practical and simple sayings. One, which is summed up in his legendary saying "as soon as you can, on the wing!", which focuses on the necessity of the fast flow of the ball from your opponent's space on the flanks. He taught me that the coach must master the art of saying important things in a simple and original way and should keep repeating it. Such communication is well accepted among players. Knowledge is always opposed to the concept of ignorance, opinion and beliefs. By looking at the training methods of the older more experienced coaches, I've learned so much.

I was fascinated as they knew exactly how to specifically give the right amount of training for all the important players. They were not slaves to the opinion that all players should train in the same way, because for them all the players weren't the same. It didn't matter to them that these players didn't train every single day like the others, taking no notice of the nasty opposing remarks. It was important to them that these "privileged" players were feeling fresh on Saturday, the day of the game, as they knew that their freshness was a key factor in winning. I also learned from them that you should have at least two players for each of the most important positions on the pitch, such as midfielders and attackers. When there are high-quality alternatives available, then you're not afraid of yellow cards or injuries. The great Croatian coach Miroslav Blazevic often uses the phrase "the one who has knowledge knows no fear"! It's so true, although the fact that bothers me is as I grow older and more experienced, I see that there is so much more I need to learn. I constantly encounter something new. It might seem funny to you, Maxi, but even today's sports equipment is no longer as it once was. Players today are much more demanding in relation to your generation. They seem to know everything, and constantly question something. Experience is very important in the formation of a coach. Experience is the path that opens the best way to gain the necessary coaching knowledge and to achieve success. Unfortunately, in the media the importance of coaching experience is far too often understated. I'm convinced the present coach of the Croatian national football team, the young and talented Niko Kovac (2015), in only ten years after his debut at the 2014 World Cup in Brazil, will become aware of how inexperienced and over ambitious he once was as a coach.

12. A persuasive technique to reach physical strength

The physical strength of players is one of the most important aspects of football training. Going back to physical training from my playing days, I still fondly remember today Maxi, how my coach used to ride a bicycle alongside us as we'd take on a twelve-kilometre run from the stadium to the nearby river. One thing's for sure - thanks to such physical training, a player can become a good runner, but doubtful he could become a highly prepared football player. So it's understandable I later spent quite a lot of time talking about the importance of a player's physical conditioning and that I've also learned something. My former club teammate, and today's coach of the strongest Iranian club Persepolis FC, Branko Ivankovic, was also taught in this very same way. Yet he was determined to come up with a fitness regime specifically tailored for football players. Something totally different from our coach on two wheels. The physical fitness of players has to be specific in relation to football. Although Ivankovic's fitness regime is varied, appealing and mainly linked to the ball, I noticed that it nevertheless falls hard on the players. This is actually a normal reaction. Players always find it hard when the training load is increased. To alleviate such reaction, for several years Branko

Ivankovic has used a motivational technique using the power of persuasion prior to training. It consists of persuading the individual players and as a group that conditional preparation is necessary to achieve the ultimate success of the team, and to keep the continuity of playing well without injury. As the season unfolds he always tries not to overload players with conditional training, yet equally not to neglect it. He never, during the season, overloads players to the limits of their physical endurance. For many years now, since working with professional clubs, a segment of physical conditioning of his team is led by a specialist, who plays an essential role in his professional team. Regardless of how much he appreciates his assistant's expertise, Branko Ivankovic still makes the call at his own discretion about the required training load of the players. His assistant, a specialist in physical training, has the green light to fully decide the best way to achieve this desired load.

13. Self-control with things out of your influence

Maxi, football really is the most beautiful sport in the world. It brings joy, pleasure, generosity, hope and even faith. Despite these sets of values, a large number of coaches, due to their enormous, constant desire to win every single game, find it a challenge to relax and enjoy its charms. I'm convinced that you're not one of them. Football would not be football if everyone constantly won. Unnecessary nervousness in these coaches usually floats to the surface while leading the team in a game. I like to observe coaches during a match. It's fascinating to see how every coach goes through the course of a game in their own different way. Some coaches are noisy and nervous. Others sit on the bench completely calm, and some are always on two feet, standing. I really do worship coaches who seem to stay calm and who can experience the play of their team stress-free. You must be wondering, Maxi, how come certain coaches manage to stay calm during a match full of twists and surprises? Well, this is because they intensively prepare before every match throughout the entire week, so there's no need to additionally influence the players during the match. In particular, no jumping and shouting in front of the bench. If the coach creates a scene and constantly shouts out comments, he creates a negative impact on the younger players, and in turn they cannot fully concentrate on the game due to the fear of making a mistake - but they constantly listen to what the coach is shouting. On the other hand, coaches who are calm can be often judged by the public and the club management as having a far too laid back attitude towards the interests of the club. This is simply not true. Within the football world, there are many coaches who cannot maintain self-control on aspects they simply cannot influence - referees, the crowd and the pitch. The simple logic indicates that this is an unnecessary exhaustion. The same applies to cases when coaches are indulged in unnecessary expert analysis and discussion with those who lack expert knowledge. Therefore, my advice to you Maxi is whenever a football 'know-it-all' wants to start a discussion with you about the tactics of the team, the game system, or even the changes you've made – you should immediately think of the wise words of the great German writer W. Goethe who once said "don't be drawn into an argument with ignorant people as you'll become ignorant yourself". Don't worry about this. People who know how to play are not sitting on the bench – they're sitting in the stands! That's how it's always been and how it'll stay. That's the beauty of football. Football isn't played because of us, but for those who look forward to the goals.

14. Noticing little things creates tactical dominance

Not everyone shares the same gift of perception. Some evaluate the gift of perception as insignificantly small. When I talk to you about coaching virtues Maxi, the gift of perception ranks highly. Lucidity of mind, observational ability and quick decision-making are not only skills needed for pilots and soldiers - but also for you coaches. After watching a 90-minute football match, a regular viewer would hardly remember all the disputable details, all the scoring opportunities and all the attacks. Unlike those, you coaches fall into the category of people who have the power of detailed observations. A coach who has developed detailed perception skills penetrates into the depths of all the missed opportunities and the opponent's tactics. The sharp power to observe the rival's game has brought victory to certain coaches, and I certainly know many who use this virtue as a good basis to explain why the match was lost. Over the last decade, coaches have paid particular attention to analysis. Together with their expert team, they involve players in the analysis of the game, analysing their rivals, their weaknesses and strengths. You wouldn't believe how important the power of perception can be when going through this in-depth process. Sometimes just noticing a minor detail can create a strategic victory. Don't fall into the trap of thinking our opponents fail to analyse us and our game. Today, everyone is aware of everything, so often little things, such as the power of perception, dominate. He who masters the trivia, knows how to master greater things. Only those who notice even the smallest mistakes can be expected not to put up with the larger ones. Small or large, important or not, coaches usually realise only after the consequences. What entails serious consequences is never a minor issue, no matter how insignificant it seems to us at that particular moment.

15. Positive atmosphere vital for success

The success of a certain club doesn't solely depend on those outstanding players and insightful coaches. It also depends on the specific atmosphere and communication culture at the club. If all these factors are combined and a family atmosphere is nurtured, the success of the club won't be far behind. Comparing previous clubs where I've played and worked, it's evident that in some, there was a lack of positive atmosphere. This was mostly due to the lack of communication culture of the people who led these clubs. Many can identify with the terms 'club culture' and 'climate', although they are two very different terms. The atmosphere shared in a sports club is a short-term situation depending on the club's leadership style and current results. A positive atmosphere draws large crowds to stadiums with a desire to have a good time, cheering for their favourites. For days, people would talk about the goals, scores and the highlights of every match. The club atmosphere, whether positive or negative, is directly influenced by the way the club is managed. It's formed mainly by those who run the club - presidents, directors, and people like you - coaches. Maxi, you might think the media plays a part in all this?

The media doesn't create the club atmosphere, it merely transfers it to the interested public. Unlike the short-term phenomenon of club atmosphere, club culture is a long-term process, created over years. It forms the environment in which players, coaches and others connected with the club, work. Part of our club culture is the wall featuring pictures of club legends in the VIP Room. Jimmy Hasty and other legends share the message of showing how much our club values its past and how much it means in terms of pride.

The working environment depends on communication, and many often neglect the fact that the club's communication is not only about discussion among the club's staff, but equally communication etiquette, the club's image, appearance, and respect for tradition. I too, as an insignificant club employee fully respect that. However, unfortunately many of our colleagues simply don't recognise that in order to bring crowds to the stadium and to significantly attract potential sponsors, not only are sports results crucial, but equally important is the tradition, a positive atmosphere and the communication climate that flows in and around the club.

16. The importance of how a coach communicates

Have you ever wondered Maxi, why certain coaches are more successful than others, even though they may have the same level of knowledge or skills? Why are they more highly valued on the sports market and simply have no trouble moving from small setups to more prestigious clubs? How come they advance and enhance their financial status and benefits, although sometimes they rarely meet the expectations of new employers? Why exactly does the media warm to them and the players enjoy training with them? What is it that sets them apart from their colleagues? Some would say it's charisma, others would add they closely follow modern trends, and perhaps somehow manage to create more of a connection with the players. It may be to do with having better contacts or knowing more influential people. Elements of the truth may be found in all of these answers. Here's a comprehensive explanation that applies to all coaches, regardless of their personality or communication profile. To succeed it's no longer enough to be recognised as a skilled, talented and result-oriented, successful coach. Today, a coach must be able to present his knowledge and the achieved results to the world, those around him and to the public. To achieve coaching success, it's really important to gain an insight into communication and marketing skills, primarily as today the public interest in sport is under a certain influence of marketing communications. The sporting public, which consists of athletes, fans, club management, spectators, the media, and sponsors don't evaluate a coach exclusively according to his professional work and the results achieved on the pitch – he's also measured as a person, according to his communication with the public. The public will always remember your results Maxi, but the way you present your personality determines the respect or disrespect you gain from the public. Every appearance is a communication opportunity – a widely spread message which creates a positive or negative impact. Among coaches there's a dominating common opinion to achieve success. The most important thing is to be a strong teacher and educator, as well as an expert in technique, tactics and the fitness regime, both in theory and in practice. I only partly agree with this opinion. Today, how a coach presents his personality and his professional work is just as important, if not more important than his actual expertise and pedagogical quality. A coach can only reach success, with the necessary qualities along with the appropriate communication in order to promote his work and sports achievements. Thanks to the know-how of marketing and communications, a coach can win sympathy and provoke emotions among the sporting public. The more emotions a coach provokes among the public, the stronger his odds of gaining sympathy and in turn, receiving better coaching job offers. Essentially, if a coach doesn't know how to present himself and his expertise - the results won't follow.

17. Every word sends a message to be remembered

A coach communicates, making direct contact with the players and those around him, on a daily basis. Personal contact with the players is of tremendous value to a coach because it enables direct two-way communication, the exchange of information, advice and everything that promotes the achievement of positive communication. Maxi, it's impossible not to communicate! Whether you speak or not, you're constantly communicating – with your appearance, tone of voice, gestures and movements. When you accidentally or deliberately ignore your players or the media - again you're communicating. Your every move, smile, greeting, your outstretched hand – these are all signals that are remembered for a long time. High quality mutual communication is one of the basic requirements of a coaching job. The coach should encourage two-way communication with his team, in order for all players to share his goals and vision. Some coaches do the majority of their communication with the captain of the team. Communication with just the captain is not enough. Communication with other members of the team is vital, as it's the only real way you can convey your enthusiasm to all your players. Individual talks with players are always very important aspects. Especially at a time when a player is going through a tough time or not performing on the pitch. Diego Maradona was once a marvellous player who could beat any opponent. But I am sure there were times during his career when he literally wanted to do everything on his own. This is impossible in football. His coach, Cesar Menotti must have got annoyed and displeased with his performance. He would have had to talk with Diego in private. Such individual conversations would have taken Diego a step forward. With his lucidity praised by the coach, he would be thrilled to listen to him and take on board his every constructive criticism. Following each interview, he would be able to regain his motivation, and we would once again see the unstoppable Maradona - the fear of the rival's goalkeeper.

18. Should you believe everything your assistants say?

Modern training and team management requires teamwork. And you Maxi, as a head coach, are only the organizer and coordinator of these activities. You have your assistants, and it's common that your daily team of associates consists of two training assistants, a doctor and a physiotherapist. Of course, this doesn't apply to your colleagues who are coaches of amateur clubs, but to the more professional teams if they can afford it. An expert team is usually made up of competent, professional people who elaborate strategic and tactical ideas, preparing players for the match. Your professional team in our club has a clearly defined goal. It's common to all and completely clear. Each member of your team knows his responsibilities and what he has to do. You realize that the team shouldn't consist of individuals who are individually doing things in their own way. The success of a team is always above the ambitions of individual team members. Do these things function like this in reality, Maxi? The establishment and operation of a professional football team is a very demanding job together with hard work. This is because different ambitions appear in different teams, as well as in yours. As a kit man, I can clearly notice when assistants, driven by personal ambition, obstruct the work of the coach. They just imagine they're better than him. Your team is a well-chosen squad. You've got high-quality loyal assistants. The worst examples for me are when assistants give support to any proposal from the head coach, and then after just one defeat, the entire blame is on him. Driven by a similar issue, the manager of a famous London Premier League club once sacked his assistant with an interesting explanation, "he was an assistant who always agreed with my opinion and suggestions. We would never disagree on anything. I don't want to keep paying him just to hear my own opinion". In a good team there are no secrets. Everyone knows what's going on, whether it's good or bad. All team members are ready and competent to express their views and differences of opinions, without fear of upsetting the team leader - the head coach. In an effort to avoid possible unnecessary conflict, it's common practice for the head coach to agree with all team members on the performance standards during the formation of his expert team. After this, team members know what the head coach and, equally, the club, expects from them. This increases the performance of the team and reduces the likelihood of conflict. In successful professional teams, there are really no secrets. Everyone knows what's happening and the potential consequences.

There's complete openness and honesty from each team

member. The unwritten rule of work of such teams is – 'together we stand and together we fall'!

19. Words or not, the coach always communicates

Personal contact is of great value to you Maxi, and for every coach. It opens the door to direct two-way communication with the players, exchanging information, feedback and everything that promotes the achievement of positive communication. It's impossible not to communicate! Whether you speak or not, you're always communicating, Maxi! Signals are sent through your appearance, tone of voice, gestures and movements.

When you deliberately or unintentionally happen to ignore players, journalists or fans, again you're communicating messages. Thanks to your communication, you'll become recognisable, as communication gives you added and unique value that sets you above the rest. Every word, every smile, greeting, and handshake with a player or fan is a message that'll be remembered for a long time. Good quality communication is one of the basic requirements of a coaching job. It's extremely important as a coach you cherish two-way communication with your team so that your goals and vision are shared among all of your players. Communication of the coach exclusively with the captain is simply not enough. You have to communicate with all members of the team so they can later transfer your messages, passion and enthusiasm to the newcomers in the team. The personal contact of the coach often depends on the attitude of interlocutors before the actual communication. The greater the cultural similarity between the coach and player in terms of origin, education, preferences and beliefs, the higher chance of successful communication. Maxi, how do you handle the new 'internet' generation of players? The new "Y" generation are not like us. This is a generation which is not used to unquestioningly accepting all the opinions and attitudes of coaches. These players have grown up alongside the Internet, Google, Twitter, Facebook and the ongoing digital world of social media. For them, there isn't the unknown. Every single thing they're interested in or have a problem with, can be found online. Specifically, for this generation they work faster and more productively than older players, yet with less recognition of the coach's authority. They search for answers about everything. Today, they're not as satisfied with the coach's answers, compared to before. When we say forty-metre sprints are ideal in training sessions for players, they look for the answer to why it's not thirty metres.

20. Speaking and listening as indispensable tools

We all talk to each other Maxi, but not all of us have managed to master the art of high-quality clear expression. Not all of us know how to engage in conversations aiming to resolve, rather than encourage conflict. Without the ability to clearly present what you know and what you want your players to be taught, you won't be able to achieve meaningful communication. You simply won't be understood. The biggest problem of most coaches is they're not aware of what they're saying and the way they come across to their players. The importance of personal exposure is increasingly becoming important and so it's important the coach knows how to communicate well with the public.

For the players to properly understand you, your communication must be complete and professional. This can only be achieved if you send a consciously planned spoken message and afterwards look to receive feedback on its acceptance and effects. The feedback you get becomes the foundation of relations between coaches and players. Feedback improves the preservation and development of high quality and effective communication. In order to be understandable to players, try to use clear, understandable language, concise sentences, words which they are familiar with and specific speech. Each coach can improve and upgrade the quality of his communication, thus preventing miscommunication among players. And how? Primarily by listening.

Do you sometimes forget the right word when explaining something, Maxi? This could mean your vocabulary is not wide enough and needs to be broadened and enriched. How can this be achieved? There's no better way to enrich your own vocabulary than reading books. Listening is also a significant element in reaching a strong level of communication. Not without reason, nature has given us all one tongue and two ears. We should listen twice as much as we talk. Unfortunately, we don't use this gift of nature as well as we should, not being aware how the quality of our lives could be improved by listening. It's simply impossible for a coach not to communicate. Equally, silence is a powerful tool. On many occasions, silence has more of an impact than any spoken word.

21. Say, point and include the players

Each training session, match, competition, or meeting with the players requires the coach's careful preparation. The way a coach conveys information regarding the opponents, the competition or the game are key. Maxi, do you know how much players actually remember from all of this? You'd be surprised! Research conducted by the Wharton School of the University of Pennsylvania in the United States reveals that the level of memorising information following a spoken presentation is only 10%, while the percentage after a presentation which includes pictures increases to 51%. After a presentation which consists of spoken content, images and including the players themselves, the level of memorising information increases to 92%. What can we conclude from this?

The spoken word of a coach has the least impact on the players. The spoken word along with visual instructions has a moderate effect. Interestingly, the coach's spoken words together with visual instructions and actively engaging the players in discussion, by far achieves the maximum effect. I strongly advise you Maxi, to enrich your preparation for competition or training with images, graphics, or even video footage. If the players are actively included in the whole story –

the success of the Lilywhites is on its way! This theoretical knowledge has been put into practice for many years by leading coaches around the world. Your assistants certainly won't be too enthusiastic about hearing this. In fact, it's them who'll have to carry and take care of all the technical equipment needed and these are sometimes difficult to transfer from the bus to the plane, and from one match to another match.

22. The power of positive thinking

"Whether you think you can, or you think you can't - you're right."

This beautiful thought of Henry Ford, the inventor of the car, confirms that by using a positive approach, anything can be achieved. The same goes for winning a match, Maxi. If we think we can do something, with a positive outlook our odds increase. A positive attitude opens a boundless source of motivation directed towards success and victory. We should always try to think positive! Most people don't take this recommendation seriously. I'm not sure whether they understand what it really means or they just see it as useless and ineffective. Aren't all of us who play football convinced that even if we've conceded a goal the game isn't over, but more so at the moment when we think we might lose? Positive thinking is a mental attitude that filters into our thoughts, words and images that contribute to growth, development and success. Positive thinking presupposes happiness, joy, health and the ability to overcome any situation. Everything our mind searches for, it finds. Positive as well as negative thinking is contagious. All of us, in one way or another, influence the people we meet, in the same way you coaches influence your players. This happens instinctively and unconsciously through our thoughts, feelings and body language. People want to be surrounded by positive people and avoid negativity! If you're positive, players will be willing to help in achieving the set goals. Negative thoughts, words and attitudes lead to dissatisfaction, failure and ultimately, disappointment. In order to become successful and popular in our work, we have to think positive, as positive thinking is conveyed to the players. The power of thinking is a powerful force that shapes our lives. This usually happens subconsciously but the process can be implemented consciously. Therefore, you have to believe in every player and expect a positive outcome to every match. With such an attitude you can't lose - only gain. If negative thoughts enter your mind, you should try to get rid of them as soon as possible and replace them with positive concepts. If you feel somewhat resistant to adopting a more positive outlook, you shouldn't give up, and continue to look for useful, good and happy thoughts inside your mind. Our positivity must be constantly obvious, especially when communicating with our players. In relation to player-coach communication, positivity is most commonly expressed through providing feedback to the players. Player feedback shouldn't include criticism, but eventually focus on expressing dissatisfaction with the players' behaviour. Feedback should be a form of analysis of activities or the behaviour of a certain player in order to help him improve. When communicating to the player it's important to always stay focused on what can be changed, rather than stick to things that might be taken as an attack on the individual's personality.

23. Self-confidence can be crucial in swaying the odds

The other day I read in the papers "Hammers manager Slaven Bilic is full of confidence before the start of the new season". Maxi, do you know what it means to be self-confident? The theory of self-esteem is defined as confidence in yourself and your possibilities. A high level of confidence is manifested through a high degree of confidence in one's own judgment, or a high opinion of one's self-worth. This means that a coach who is full of confidence is one who believes completely in his own professional knowledge, skills and abilities. We can all agree with that, can't we? Such a coach always, both directly and indirectly, transfers his confidence to the team, motivating the players to exploit their potential to the fullest. A confident coach transfers a positive attitude and spreads optimism among players. Coaches who are full of confidence are not averse to risk-taking and taking responsibility in the most critical moments of the game. They accept each difficult situation as a challenge. Self-confidence is certainly one of the significant factors distinguishing successful from less successful coaches. Most coaches have excellent technical knowledge, but often fail to cross the border to genuine excellence. Why? One of the key reasons is that they're not sure of their abilities and capabilities, not using them at critical moments when it's most needed for the team. They never take risks, always opting for a safer option. You're probably wondering where exactly the problem lies? In the head, Maxi. It's all in the head.

Coaches with low confidence must overcome their psychological barriers and start believing in themselves, in their knowledge, skills and abilities. It might mean abandoning the usual security, but for sure, if we don't change ourselves, we won't progress. So I'll repeat once again that coaches who have a far better chance on the road to success speak steadily, behave properly, look appropriate, and are always in a good mood. Simply, in a nutshell, those who've mastered the skill of verbal and non-verbal communication radiate with confidence, before they've even said their first word.

24. Always 'fair play'

All of us who are involved with sport, either as coaches, players, staff, fans, or sponsors, should have a highly developed awareness of ethics and ethical behaviour. Ethics in sport dictates the relationship we have with ourselves and with others in a way that everybody is satisfied. 'Fair play' is one of the most important categories of ethics in sport. The founder of the modern Olympic Movement, Pierre de Coubertin, firmly believed "fair play" had a special place in sport and ethics. Did you know Maxi, that the Declaration of Human Rights of the United Nations states: "All human beings are born free and equal in dignity and rights". This is a big deal. Coaches should teach this to players from an early age, so, regardless of being in competition or in conflict, they'd always remember this statement. 'Fair play' and the fight to stamp out racism in sport should be seen as the greatest moral value of sport, as a guarantee of fair competition, acceptance of the rules and respect for the sport. To respect 'fair play' means to respect and abide by its rules. In a club where 'fair play' is fostered, you'll always find honesty, safety, and a passion for justice. To behave fairly with your opponent means to be tolerant and calm. The opposite of 'fair play' represents fraud and cheating, inconsistency, violence, hatred, discrimination and disrespecting the rules. Coaches whose only philosophy is to be top of their league, often dare to question fairness and violate the rules of the game. 'Fair play' is not just a sports term, it's also a synonym for reasonable behaviour in everyday life. Unfortunately, and you well know this Maxi, the reality is not always in the spirit of 'fair play'. Within many clubs, coaches are met with hatred, jealousy, gossip and disrespect. Evidence for this can be easily found. There are coaches who'll try to win at all costs, even to sacrifice their defensive player, instructing him to injure the opposing attackers, regardless of the consequences - clearly an instruction to physically injure his opponent. There are also examples around the world where in major competitions, famous players, contrary to the rules, score a goal using their hand, and then deny it ever happened. The ideals of 'fair play' should constantly shine in the work of a coach. A successful coach appreciates sport, the game and the athletes regardless of skin colour and religion, follows the rules and strictly plays fairly. He knows that it's the only right way to practise sport and the only satisfaction guaranteed after competition and training. So, Maxi, respect 'fair play', always strive to do your best at every training session and competitive game, accept and support the sports rules and the message it represents. A coach, player or team whose commitment, desire to win with creativity and ability are strong, should always be congratulated at the end of the match, regardless of the outcome.

25. Each crisis means an opportunity

Today I'd like to start with a story, Maxi. The famous Croatian coach, Drazen Besek, had just taken over the reins of Chinese club Shanghai Shenhua. He was in the back of a taxi on his way from his hotel to the stadium. Along the route he spotted a giant billboard with two big Chinese letters. He was intrigued so he asked the taxi driver what they meant. The taxi driver explained that together they mean - a crisis, but if read individually, the first means danger and the second, opportunity. Within European culture, in which the two of us grew up, a crisis in a term is traditionally seen as a problem or an obstacle. Undoubtedly, Chinese traditional culture is far more creative compared to Europe! For the Chinese, a crisis means just as much danger as a good opportunity. Due to the nature of their work, coaches work with crisis situations on a daily basis and therefore need to be familiar with crisis communication. Two defeats in a row, the absence of the crowd favourite from the starting eleven are issues that can easily lead the coach to a crisis situation. Statistics show that coaches who failed to communicate well during a crisis situation were often let go in just a few days, tarnishing their reputation on the way. Of course, there are positive examples when coaches strategically manage the crisis thanks to excellent communication.

Having learned this Chinese story about my friend, I want you to know that every single crisis for a coach always means, not danger, but a new opportunity. The crisis is an opportunity for a coach to obtain media coverage which is otherwise hard to reach. Maxi, you should always be prepared for a crisis situation and the media interest that it attracts. You're a public figure and you actively participate in the public life of the community. So it's normal to be accountable for your work and, likewise, the media interest you attract in a crisis situation is completely understandable. Media experts point out that in a crisis, the first 24 hours are crucial. During this period, the pressure from the media towards the coach is at its peak, as the public curiosity begins to grow. The way a coach communicates in the first 24 hours reveals how capable and trained he is to deal with the challenge. A results crisis in sport is a normal thing that eventually every coach needs to deal with. Weren't you hit quite hard not too long ago with a defeat against Cork at Oriel Park? How can a coach handle the situation following a string of poor results? Coaches shouldn't deny their responsibility. Taking responsibility doesn't mean recognition of guilt, which, unfortunately, many coaches fail to grasp. Coaches must understand the media's hunger for information. They don't need to hide away from the media, turning off their mobile phones. Based on my own experience, I would strongly suggest avoiding press conferences in the first couple of days after the outbreak of the crisis. Why? Communication via press conferences puts every coach in front of a 'firing squad' with the attack of all sorts of questions, some quite uncomfortable and awkward, so it's far better to avoid them. During a crisis period, the smartest advice is to give affirmative statements, without further excuses or blame, or to use a positive notion to overshadow fresh negative news. I would recommend, if your club gives the 'green light', completing your expert team with a communications specialist. He'll certainly know what to do and greatly advise you on how to communicate during a crisis. Don't forget that all of you coaches are under quite a lot of pressure and anxiety levels are high during a crisis situation, and your thoughts are more or less subjective.

26. The managerial merry-go-round

In most football nations, including here in Ireland, after a series of consecutive defeats, it's common practice to see a change of head coach. Why has this preferred solution by club management become the norm, Maxi? Usually because after the coach comes in, the result-oriented effect of the team immediately increases. But, in most cases, this growth trend is short-lived. During the first weeks following the change of the coach, players closely watch the new one. They're obedient, trying to create an impact, with maximum engagement. On the other hand, the new coach wants to be seen in the most positive light possible. He wants to show his knowledge and competence to the players, and to gain their trust. He searches for the ideal team, asking players to fight for their position etc. Players, who once had certain credibility with the former coach, become just equal contenders for the first 11 with the new one. Once the first team squad has crystallized, there's a time of stabilization. Those who don't feature in the first "11" or "18", immediately become the opposition of the coach. If in the new coach, the team doesn't recognize his "strength" or the person who can help achieve their goals, he won't do well. If however, a new coach manages to impose his expertise, integrity and approach on the players, his position becomes stable and he can expect a competitive breakthrough. Why? Players surrender themselves unconditionally to the coach they've accepted. They warm to his decisions and his method of managing the team, which leads to long-term success. Players' belief in the coach's competence can greatly influence the overall strength of the team. Nevertheless, if the results turn, and things don't go the way of the club, a change is on the cards. Your bags should always be ready, right Maxi?

27. What do people think of you?

Have you ever been haunted by the thought: "What people think of me", Maxi? "What would they say if I picked Roy instead of Paul?" If you aim to become a top coach, you'll never bother with what people say about your work. You should worry about what your conscience says. To follow your conscience means you're a coach with a strong character. The largest obstacle in building a strong character is the fact that it can't be built overnight. This is always a slow process. Maturing ourselves takes the hard work of a lifetime. Today's major obstacle in building a strong character is the continued fast pace of life, and running after achievements of material value. Within a blink of an eye, a huge number of coaches can tell you the names the first eleven of their opposing teams, but in terms of their own character, they'll struggle to say a few words as they've probably failed to recognise who they actually are. Character cannot be built without knowing ourselves, without learning and constant development. This is normal as success can't be reached without victims and sacrifices. The best example of this is the coaching profession. Getting up early in the morning ready for training, having lunch, then back to the training pitch once again. During the evening more match analysis, training preparation for the next day, and so on - day after day. It's the same with our character.

To build your own character, you need to invest a huge amount of persistence and premeditated work. Don't ever complain or justify why you're this or that, why you're passionate, temperamental, or have a short fuse. Your seemingly untamed passion and fiery temperament can be nurtured with practice. Everything is simply a matter of desire, exercise and training. Those that give up easily, usually say "I'm this way by nature. That's how I was born". This certainly isn't true. To back this up, I always remember the late president of the club where I started my career. After drinking just a few glasses of alcohol, he'd unfortunately turn into an unpleasant and confrontational beast. As a very clever man, he immediately recognised his drinking issues and worked hard to address them. He then gave up alcohol. Even today, I admire the positive strength of his character. Everything can be achieved if there's a real desire. Unlike him, it took me, unfortunately, ten years to finally realise I had a problem with alcohol. Regardless of this, today I'm happy and content, so it's never too late for a man to become the man he wants to be!

28. The person I am

Regardless of the level of competency or expertise of a coach, the players and sports public see him firstly, as a person. If they don't like him as a person, they won't like him as a coach, despite his knowledge and skills. Besides giving a positive answer to the question "What kind of an expert am I? ", a coach is also expected to answer the question "What kind of person am I? ". Maxi, just like many coaches, I'm sure you've invested a lot of time and effort in your professional development. Do you know how much time you've devoted to your personal development? Believe me when I say that only development in both segments results in achieving a successful coaching career! As coaches, you all tend to invest additional time and money to enhance your knowledge about technique, tactics, and physical training, yet only of a few of you are willing to go ahead and invest in personal development. Equally, without having both sets of expertise, you can't become a strong and successful coach. Talking about a coach, how many times have I heard players say: "He's a great coach! He knows everything. But God forbid if he ever leads the training session. He doesn't know how to communicate. He's a really tough person and unable to cooperate. He's always right, shouting and never listens to anyone"!

The professional quality of these coaches will never come to light as they've never learned fundamental human communication skills. A coach will never become successful based only on his knowledge of technique, tactics and physical preparation. If you want to become a successful coach Maxi, along with your expertise, you have to master and fine tune your communication skills. You have to open the doors of your spirituality. The adoption of communication skills and the impact on people is extremely important for coaches, as well as the kind of impression it leaves. The same applies to players. Players, who develop in just a professional capacity, fail to achieve the best results. Top players become those who, along with having the talent and sports skills, understand and appreciate human relationships in the team.

29. The crucial role of a coach in conflict situations

Coaches don't like conflict. They'll do everything they can to avoid tension in the changing rooms. Naturally conflict with players or colleagues isn't good at all, and should be avoided at all costs. No matter how bad things become, sometimes the consequences for the team can be useful. There's never complete harmony in the team. Football is a game where only eleven actually play. The apparent team harmony only lasts for as long as the team is winning. With the first defeat, along come the first signs of tension. The role of a coach in a conflict situation is therefore crucial. He has to use his authority and competence to maintain the unified spirit of his team. What does that actually mean? This means a coach must be decisive and be open to cooperation and compromise. If through conflict a coach turns out to be in the wrong, he has to be reasonable and willing to accept his mistake, and ready to listen and consider a better proposal. It's obvious that different situations require different procedures from coaches. Maxi, I know you well and I know you're not one of those coaches who wants to always be right, who has to win in every situation. In your career, were you ever in a situation where your players' suggestions to resolving a problem were better than yours?

A well sought quality of a coach is the willingness to accept things, even when he may not be pleased with it. I know it's a terrible kick to the ego, especially when you hear it from a player. When you listen to something that you don't like, don't immediately defend or deny it and try to stay away from sarcasm. In conflict situations, always trying to emphasise the importance of the contribution of the entire team in order to achieve the club's goals is always more important than the achievement of the individual targets of disgruntled players or coaches.

30. Don't justify defeat

"We wouldn't have lost if Daryl Morgan had played against Cork." Looking for excuses after a defeat is a desperate move, Maxi! Just like you, many coaches want to justify their failure with the recent challenges they've faced. Do you think a problem, such as Daryl Morgan not playing, is a valid excuse for the team's defeat? Have you ever thought that maybe you as a coach are the one most accountable for the defeat? Why not find an appropriate replacement for Daryl? You didn't find a replacement for Daryl, but you immediately found a good excuse in his absence. It seems to me that failure against Cork was set in advance, even before the game started. I'll tell you an interesting story I read in the papers on the subject. Once you hear it, you'll never look for an excuse after defeat again. When Dwight Eisenhower, the supreme commander of the Allied forces in World War II, left his military service he became the rector of the University of Columbia in New York. One day a student approached him, asking to change the exam time, because he wasn't feeling well. He asked to postpone the scheduled time because he simply wanted more time to prepare better. Eisenhower asked: "Have you been unwell perhaps?" The student then replied: "I wasn't sick, but I've been feeling bad," replied the student. "Dear friend," he answered as he turned towards the other students, "Most of the great and significant actions in the world were done by people who had been in a bad mood or even sick. Due to being unwell some were even more hard-working, as they felt their time was numbered to achieve their plans. So I openly say: if me and my soldiers had done whatever we liked, things that only made us happy, we would never have won the Second World War. However, since we were all completely committed to the hard work we had to do, and persevered in severe difficulties, we ultimately won freedom for the whole world". I'm convinced Eisenhower's message is a good example of how every difficulty can and must be transformed into a surge of motivation. It's not easy, but that is precisely the secret of success. Successful people don't allow themselves to be broken by all sorts of problems. They use them as motivation towards the goals they set. It doesn't matter whether you've let in a goal, whether you're down to ten men, or even if your best players are injured. It's important you stay in the game. You need to have the drive to want to score and to win. In football, we face constant challenges and ultimately it's up to you and your players to make the decision to surrender and give up - or win. In football it's specifically these difficulties faced by coaches which should become the highest possible motivation. So, the next time you're thinking of justifying yourself, bite your tongue and simply continue to do what you are doing. You'll see that the 'expected' defeat will turn into victory.

31. The greatness of a coach shines through in tough times

Human greatness is best seen in difficult situations. The coaching profession is a perfect reflection of this. In times of challenges, conflicts and hardships our true nature is best expressed. It's not easy to be great both in victory and defeat. What's the best way to react following defeat? What should you do when the media, fans or club's board pile on the pressure and swoop down on you like hornets? Hardly any coach during tough times can think about stress. You usually start focusing on stress when you begin to feel the first signs of health problems. So, what exactly are the symptoms of stress? You usually notice certain physical symptoms such as feeling discomfort, fast breathing, a pounding heart and higher levels of anxiety. Maxi, after we lost at Oriel Park against Cork on Friday, did you feel any of these stress symptoms? "I knew what I was in for in front of the press. Before talking to you, heading to the mandatory post-match press conference, I felt I was heading towards a firing squad of journalists who were thirsty for my blood. Just before going to the press room, I hadn't had enough time to put together any sort of analysis of the match, and to reflect in peace about the specific reasons for the defeat. Just like many things in life, solutions can be solved by exercise and training. Thanks to your suggestion, Yuri, at a DkIT seminar on stress management I attended, I managed to adopt a few breathing techniques. With these in mind, I arrived at the press conference very calm and self-composed. During the press conference, I reduced the scope and content of the information that I would otherwise generously share with the journalists. Using this approach, and without giving names and pointing the finger, I reduced the window of opportunity for journalists to throw in additional questions and create bombastic headlines. Believe me, Yuri, it wasn't easy for me to come home and listen to the news with one of my off-the-wall statements which I'm sure caused offence to someone. Not only that, such a statement would spark a whole host of reactions, so instantly, I became the topic of conversation for the entire week. Not to mention the next training session addressing the tense players who were casually mentioned in my statement."

So you're right Maxi, I'm so proud of you. You see it's all a matter of practice and working on yourself. Success, happiness and inner peace can't be achieved by itself. Everything comes from the right, positive thinking.

32. No success without parental cooperation and support

Throughout my footballing life, especially now since I've been working as a kit man, Maxi, I regularly meet parents and explain what would be the best thing for their budding little football players. I think a child shouldn't be introduced to the training process before the age of seven. The most important thing at pre-school age is to develop affection towards the sport and training through the game. This process takes more than a single coach. It takes a number of coaches who work with children at the earliest age. It's really important a coach knows the child's parents, because there's no success without parental cooperation and support. All parents want the best for their child and at no time must they feel their child isn't in good hands.

Speak to parents often, as they should be aware that it's not only important for their child to become a good football player, but equally a good person. Often, this isn't easy as there are parents who simply don't understand the sport, who already see their child playing for Celtic. The idea behind the concept of each serious football school, along with the football training and development, should be the mandatory completion of secondary education. During this time, young footballers, together with their school obligations, should be involved in training or a competitive program four to five times a week. Often coaches and parents are thrilled with their child's outstanding ball skills, declaring him a great potential talent and future football star. They quickly forget perfect ball skills isn't the only talent a child must have to become a top-flight footballer. Footballing talent also consists of perseverance, character, speed and strength. I also remember an opposite case when a fourteen-year-old's parents wanted their son to join one of our under-age teams. He was tall, extremely fast and totally besotted with football. Much to his and his parents regret, the difference in controlling the ball between him and the older players was dramatic. Today this shows us, Maxi, that any attempt to involve a child in the serious football world after the age of ten is simply unrealistic. Preferably, as soon as possible, young players should be involved in working alongside senior players as this is the fastest way for them to mature. It's strongly suggested that you often introduce the occasional talented junior to your training sessions and friendly matches. This is a very good way for young players to adapt as soon as possible to senior football and its demands.

33. Is quality essential in determining the price of a coach?

It's very difficult and complex to evaluate a coach. What do you think Maxi, was the reason for engaging you at the Lilywhites - was it your quality or was it something else? Even though the public believes the quality of a certain coach is the most important factor to determine his value, in reality this is only partially true. The decision of football clubs and associations whether or not to hire a certain coach is made based on personal imaginary values, the opinions of the media, his perception in the media and his achieved results. The price of a coach is negotiated on the basis of his expertise and achieved results, but this isn't decisive in agreeing the final price. The actual quality is only part of the subjective assessment of the one who is actually hiring. An important component of the judgment is the image of the coach or the public image formed by the respective coach. Football trends show that forming a price estimation for certain coaches is based primarily on the market conditions at a given moment. The expertise, results, and appropriate licence are all considered to be obligatory. In determining the final price, the way in which a coach presents his knowledge and personality in public is essential. A coach, who has built a stronger public image, generally achieves a higher market price. What does this mean in practice? This means that regardless of someone having the same level of knowledge and skills as Roy Keane, the club will still go ahead and hire Roy Keane, for sure.

34. Knowledge is vital for success

It's often said that a coach is a man who says on Friday he knows what will happen on Saturday, while on Sunday he's explaining why it didn't happen. The coaching profession is no longer exclusively linked with the pitch, the individual or even the team. Today, alongside the work on the technical and tactical elements, a coach has to communicate with the media, sponsors and fans. He also needs to show to the players his own example on how to behave, how to appear and how to represent yourself to the public. Knowledge of communication and marketing skills can help every coach. Don't forget Maxi, the mere fact that someone is a good coach is no longer a guarantee of success. Therefore, you must constantly develop yourself. Knowledge is vital for success in any business, especially in a profession that involves working with people. Fortunately, we're in a time where more and more high-quality, educated coaches with a positive image are in high demand. Although they're not cheap, they don't have a problem finding coaching positions. Why couldn't you become one of them Maxi? By investing in knowledge, you're investing indirectly in your image. Although there's no major difference in creating the image of players and coaches, there are some specifics in creating the image of a coach. In order to become successful in any field, you have to be distinguished and set yourself apart from the others. Good communication of the coach opens the door to creating a positive image. Your decision on insisting everyone wears the same clothes is to be commended as this is also a form of communication. The uniform worn by the players creates a sense of a club member's security and a feeling of belonging to a group.

35. Becoming a brand increases competitiveness

Thanks to television, football has become global. It's visible in every corner of the planet. Wherever there's an audience, there are always sponsors and advertisers who swiftly recognize the marketing value of sport. All this combined creates the global popularity of top athletes and coaches. The marketing value of coaches as public figures, has a strong impact on people's behaviour, especially when it comes to influencing consumers. From a marketing point of view, coaches themselves have become a kind of recognizable sports brand. Why should you be interested in becoming a brand Maxi? A brand is a tool that increases the competitiveness of a coach in the sport's market. A brand can be the decisive difference between coaches of the same level of quality. The strength of the coach as a brand simplifies the decision-making process, reduces risk and reflects the quality and high expectations. For example, football coach Pat Fenlon is today a recognized coaching brand in Ireland, which means that in the sports market his value is higher than his assistant Stephen Bradley. The difference between a 'branded' coach and an 'ordinary' coach is that brands aren't created on the pitch, but in people's perceptions. The most famous brand in the world is Coca-Cola. The company name represents a certain image and identity, as well as the product itself. What would coke be without its name? Just one more in a series of flavoured drinks on the shelves. Today, there are lots of excellent coaches, and for the most part, clubs engage those who have developed their own identity and image - those who have become a coaching brand. We all know about Brendan Rodgers, Arsene Wenger, 'Pep' Guardiola, Jose Mourinho, Martin O'Neill, Stephen Kenny, Slaven Bilic and Branko Ivankovic. All of these coaches have become brands, some stemming from the world stage and others locally. Famous coaches as public figures have a strong impact on people's behaviour, and are often engaged by large companies to promote and endorse their products. In the sports world there have been examples of top-level sports coaches who earn far more from sponsorship deals than from what they earn on the football pitch.

36. Do coaches earn too much?

We've now come to a touchy subject, Maxi. Do football coaches earn too much? Hmmm... The fact is coaches who work with children earn far too little. I'll try to express my opinion by sharing a story. When you've heard it, you'll understand my take on whether coaches earn too much. *One day, a rich merchant decided to commission an interesting painting from a painter. This specific painting was supposed to represent a rooster in the most perfect way possible. A few years went by since his order, with no sight nor word of the painter. As his anxiety and uncertainty grew, he went to discover what exactly had happened to the painter. He eventually found the painter, but there was no painting. The painter invited the merchant to sit down and started to work on his request. In 15 minutes the painting of the rooster was complete. It was beautiful. A real masterpiece. The merchant was sincerely struck by its beauty. When it was time to pay for the painting, the merchant was stunned at the huge sum the artist dared to ask for a job completed in such a short time. He was so angry, he refused to pay. The painter then took the merchant to his room and showed him a pile of paper the height of a man. On each piece of paper was a painting of a rooster. "I've been painting these for three years to practise. Thanks to this, I've gained the skills to paint this divine, perfect painting in such a short time. And so I have to get paid for my work during the long preparation time," explained the painter. The merchant was convinced the painter was right and paid him for the painting.* It's the same thing in your coaching career, Maxi. It takes years and years of training and perseverance in order to eventually gain a well-deserved reward, which means charging for your long-term hard work.

37. Use every free moment to relax

I partially agree with you Maxi, when you say that success is based on hard work and complete dedication to the job. My years of experience give me the right to say you need to devote time to yourself and to your family. The older and more experienced I get, the more I stick to it. Unlike before, I don't spend my whole day working. I began to devote more of my time to myself and my family. I've noticed that since making the change, my body and mind are constantly in shape. My philosophy in life is not to outdo others, but my previous achievements. And in order to be able to work on myself, I take advantage of every free moment to relax. Only now do I understand why my late father George kept on saying: "Rest more and don't be constantly at work. When you relax your worries will disappear on their own, whether you want them to or not". The most common moments of relaxation are those spent with family and friends. It's interesting to note that the best strategies and ideas from Croatian football coach Branko Ivankovic actually emerged during his time drinking tea with friends and his brothers, who are his most objective critics. So, Maxi, as my father advised me, I do the same to you, urging you not to miss the opportunity to dedicate at least one hour per day to yourself. There are many ways to do this.

It entirely depends on your mood and circumstances. Perhaps just spending time with family members or a visit to places you're interested in like an art gallery or museum. Maybe buy a ticket for a concert. Reading books or watching movies might be your thing. Something simple like our football chat over tea may be just what you need. Often this can be just talking with those close to you. These are various ways to recharge your batteries. An hour every day devoted purely to yourself will help clear your mind. Dedication to yourself will allow you to get rid of negative thoughts and become creative, calm and self-collected.

38. The public fail to understand why coaches are attacked

Maxi, I heard that on Friday, after the match, you exchanged harsh words with our president. What happened? His words seemed to catch you off guard. I know it's hard for you to forget that conversation and to look back at it with objective eyes. Do you know why you can't get over what happened? It's because you take it too personally. When you take things too personally, you're not able to look at the situation objectively. As soon as you get into conflict with someone and feel the surge of violent reactions, you have to learn to develop a shield in order to reject the negative attitude and harsh words directed at you. The secret to avoid unnecessary controversy and negative reaction is to be aware that in most cases people don't understand why they're being attacked, so you have to forgive them for that, and not react negatively. Or maybe you're convinced that our president understands the tactics? Coping with personal attacks was a lesson I learned at the beginning of my short coaching career. The club where I used to work had a weak team, but my president believed we simply didn't have such a strong team for a long time. After just one defeat he spoke about me in front of the press, saying that I didn't know how to manage the players, although he never actually played football, nor did he understand the game. Rather than let it go, as a coach I reacted violently. Coincidentally, our debate was observed by the club's psychologist. Once we were alone, instead of reacting and defending my argument, the psychologist advised me that in a case like this, I never need to prove to another he's wrong and especially not the president of the club. Initially this dampens the mood of everyone present and also I wouldn't gain the upper hand and be regarded as smarter. Why not leave a man convinced that he's right and why embarrass him in front of other people? Avoid situations like these, Maxi - especially with our president.

39. Coaches need to mature

A coach on a mission to succeed needs to understand the nature of team leadership. The ability to lead a team is determined by the greatness of the coach. Leading a professional sports team is a complex process that involves mastering an array of skills - from general knowledge, professional expertise, and pedagogy to communication. All these skills are barely acquired in a short period of time. Certainly not over night, but with time and patience, all the necessary knowledge and skills can be gained by every coach. Every one of these skills can be learned and improved upon. Do freshly picked grapes turn into wine in just one day? Time is needed for grapes to mature. It's the same with football coaches. Figuratively speaking, coaches also need to mature. Like many well-known and recognized coaching names, before you flourish you have to work in the shade. Maxi, how long were you only an assistant at Shels? You were there up until the moment your chance came to you. Doors open to anyone who's willing to take it. Like diamonds that are created under huge pressure, so coaches are created through many ordeals. Young coaches are often impatient and want to make their way into a great club overnight. Some often get lost and simply disappear from the coaching scene although many are highly talented. Why? The lack of experience, wisdom and humility. The three virtues that can only be developed over time. Yes Maxi, these are very important elements to gain success in coaching, along with other necessary qualities and maturity.

40. Is polite behaviour a sign of weakness?

When you knocked on the door, Maxi, it reminded me of something from the start of my coaching career. Not even two months had passed since the day I took over the Croatian football club, NK *Varteks*. During a training session, the physio approached me with the message that the president of the club was waiting for me in his office. The tone of his voice and facial expression signalled something wasn't quite right. I was prepared for the worst. Tea was brought into the room and, without any small talk, we got straight to the nitty-gritty. "Coach, they tell me you're too polite in leading the team. You have to know that the players are bastards. You need to be firm and dynamic with them". Despite being alone, I was taken aback by his remark. I reacted like lightning with a counter-question "Normally, you expect me to knock on the door before entering your office, and as I come in it's normal to say 'Hello, how are you?'. What would you think of me if I'd entered your office without even knocking, without a greeting, saying 'Hi, how can I help?'. Is civilized behaviour to my players a sign of my weakness - a sign that I'm soft?" After my energetic and impulsive reaction, the club president was left speechless and then apologized to me. Maxi, this story is a classic example of how a civilized and democratic leadership style has nothing to do with strength and discipline. We all know that leadership styles may vary. In theory, there are two styles widely accepted: autocratic and democratic. They are often considered as mutually exclusive. You belong to one or the other. But is it really like this? Can they both be integrated? I strongly believe they can! This is precisely what many coaches do. When working with your players you should always be a gentleman, but in terms of the way you lead the team, a balance is needed. If necessary, you need to be firm, soft, flexible and adaptable and use the style which seems the most appropriate at the time. Your team leadership style depends very much upon the particular situation, the culture of the environment in which you perform and the individual personalities of certain players. Asians, unlike Europeans, perceive criticism in a very emotional and devastating way. The criticism shared has to be tactful as it's very sensitive to criticise players in front of other members of the team. All issues with Asian players should be resolved in private, with lots of individual face-to-face discussion. Most coaches, who start work in Asia aren't aware of the subtleties and so often scandal is caused by their inappropriate statements. This is particularly true in China, Korea and Japan - Asian countries where the pressure to succeed is immense.

41. Reacting to public criticism

How many times have you found yourself in a situation feeling hurt due to criticism, Maxi? I'm sure you've often thought for days about the harsh words or the sharp pen of a journalist. The eternal question that follows coaches is how to handle criticism. The answer depends on whether the criticism is justified and who it's from, although there are some coaches among you who are convinced no criticism whatsoever is justified.

If the criticism is justified, and expressed by people who know your work, you have to seriously take it into consideration. Opinions of people who don't know you, don't need to be regarded as so relevant, as they criticise the person they imagine you to be. They've created an opinion about you through media writings or your public appearances, either positive or negative, so you must understand this is something you simply cannot influence. I think every coach as a public figure should accept well in advance that his life or the work he does is going to provoke varied reactions in the public eye, which often end up with unfounded and inaccurate opinions. These are undeniable facts you have to be aware of, Maxi. If you struggle to accept them, you'll be forced to constantly fight a losing battle. So, avoid correcting people in order to change their false beliefs, because it simply doesn't make sense. It's better to keep your head and save your time and energy for the people you can understand and enjoy communicating with. Sometimes it's even better to let people wallow in their ignorance, when their attitude has nothing in common with the truth, than spend time and effort on unnecessary additional explanations. Everyone is entitled to a false belief, but equally you have the right to ignore such false beliefs. The public therefore has a right - not to have the right, but that doesn't mean they need to explain every wrong opinion or attitude. In my country, Croatia, there's a beautiful saying perfect for this - "If on your way, you look back at every barking dog, you'll never reach your goal". So, Maxi, I suggest you don't bother with the critical opinions of people you don't know or the only thing left for you is to continue banging your head against the wall, wondering how your beautiful coaching job has turned into a nightmare.

42. Never regard sports journalists as enemies

You're not satisfied with the article in Saturday's Independent? Don't despair! Maxi, journalists are just people like everyone else, with all their strengths and weaknesses. Journalists have the right to be wrong, it's just that their errors are visibly exposed to the public, unlike others. Many of them have their own pet coaches as well as those they don't particularly respect. At the start of my coaching career, I was also extremely sensitive to the opinion of other people and media criticism, especially after I had a few drinks. When I read a negative article about me, I often called the journalist who had written it to try to explain that he was wrong. My resentful pride demanded explanations and evidence for the way this article had been written. I wasn't aware that this would mean adding fuel to the fire. Today, when I look back, my responses seem amusing. Life experience has taught me that it's much more important to know how to remain indifferent to criticism than to constantly explain to people that they've attacked you with no right. The same applies to the relationship with the media. After so many years of working in sport, I'm aware that probably more than half of those who bought the paper that day didn't even pay attention to the article that made me so angry. And those who did actually read it, I imagine understood the article in the same way it appeared to me. Today I realise that people don't think so much about others, but mostly themselves. It worries them more not to have taken their dog for a walk than whether the coach of their favourite players made a ludicrous substitution during the match. I'm also aware it takes a lot of time, effort, hard work, tolerance and patience to develop mutual trust and respect between coaches and journalists.

Maxi, I would suggest you meet media representatives in person as it makes cooperation easier. Don't be suspicious of the media. Most journalists are highly committed and take pride in their work. Sport journalists have to be seen as an essential partner in the joint venture. Not as enemies, not even those you've had a bad experience with in the past. You must be aware of the public eye's great interest in football, as well as coaches. You also have to accept there'll always be someone hoping to criticise your work unfairly. When you take this inevitable fact on board, life will get easier. Keep trying hard, do the best you can and just smile at the comments, complaints, tiny digs and criticism. This, by far, is the best recipe. In the past, we can find various examples of different coach behaviour towards journalists. In the early eighties, the coach of the Italian national team Enzo Bearzot accepted his players' initiative when they defended themselves from the sly journalistic comments by simply ignoring the media. This is where the accepted notion "Silencio Stampa" was coined - not giving a statement to the press. This wasn't just within Italy as it was later adopted across the world and became a tactic accepted by many coaches. I don't support such an attitude of coaches and athletes towards journalists, because it's counterproductive. Avoiding statements doesn't mean a breakdown in communication, it's just a breakdown in talking with the media. Messages transmitted by silence, speak a lot more, but one thing is certain – they don't bring people together.

43. Coaches on the rise or fall - never refuse journalists

Thanks to television, sport has become a global game as sports coaches have transformed into celebrities due their regular TV appearances. We live in an age where coaching careers are increasingly influenced by the media. Although we're told most of your fellow coaches only live on results and success, this is only partly the truth, Maxi. These days, this is no longer enough. Today, a successful coach, along with his professional knowledge and results on the pitch has to have a level of popularity and a personal image. Those who achieve popularity know how to promote their work which can be done easily through the media. You must never forget the importance of the media, Maxi, even when you're at a low point, likewise when you're doing well. The media is represented by journalists who are the link between coaches and the interested public. They're the ones who transmit the coach's thoughts and shape the image of the coach in the public eye. Why do coaches attract the attention of the media? Firstly, they're public figures, and also the audience wants to hear expert feedback on certain moves in the game. Journalists love interesting, witty and charming interlocutors. Among those who deviate from the stereotype is your coaching colleague Jose Mourinho. Not a day goes by without a statement from the special one, not only for the English, but also Irish and other international media. Journalists prefer easy-to-reach and available coaches. If you avoid the press, if contact with them becomes a burden, and if you're bothered by certain questions and criticism, journalists will eventually avoid you too. Talking of relationships between coaches and journalists, I always think of an interesting remark by a friend of mine, a sports journalist - "he was never refused by a coach who was at the start of his career and equally who had a problem".

He was always refused by the coaches who at some point felt powerful and untouchable, forgetting that the wheel of fortune constantly turns and can one day find themselves back at the bottom. The third thing that attracts reporters is the coach's expertise. Knowledge can fascinate everyone, including journalists.

The media is the long arm of the public and the soul of the fans, and that's the way you have to experience it, Maxi. Naturally, the media will sometimes be of harm, but it will also provide a good opportunity for free promotion. It often depends on you and your relationship with the media. It's simple - seize the media Maxi!

44. Energy and emotion transformed into calm reflection

Several times already, Maxi we've spoken about how the profession of a sports coach is constantly faced with crisis situations and how it's very important how to deal with them. As I often like to take advantage of every available opportunity to learn something new, I took the opportunity as a kit man to join a seminar on coach behaviour in times of crisis, which was held at our club premises. Not even two years had passed when the knowledge gained that day was paid back to the club with interest. How was this done? Due to our three key players getting injured, our club unexpectedly found itself among the clubs which were fighting hard to stay up in the First Division. No one could predict that the fight for First Division survival would be coupled with our coach Alfred Heinl's battle with the officials, the critically minded public and disgruntled fans. I was desperate as at the time, I couldn't help Heinl. When he was already exhausted from his unfair battle which he had got himself into, I thought of the seminar. I asked our junior coach, Miroslav Bradaska, who was also present at the seminar, to share with him some of the techniques to handle crisis situations. Bradaska approached Heinl very timidly, afraid that he wouldn't accept his help. Luckily our experienced coach wasn't vain at all and immediately accepted the help, knowing he had nothing to lose - only gain. It was calmly explained that there was no need to panic. A positive attitude can quickly reverse the situation no matter how dark and gloomy it appears. Bradaska explained that in case of possible relegation from the First Division, Heinl wouldn't be declared an enemy of the state, and that no one was in fact going to shoot him. The worst thing that could happen was he'd lose his well-paid job. The wise and experienced coach was well aware of the possible consequences and was reconciled with the fact that, if needed, he'd accept them. After learning from Bradaska what he'd learned at the seminar, Heinl seemed calmer than before. There were no more outbursts at the matches, nor did he enter into debates with the officials. He was no longer obsessed with poor results and neither did he lose his nerves due to negative media headlines. From conversations he had had with Bradaska and further on, all his energy and emotions were directed to forging strategies which could help our team being saved from relegation. I don't know if you followed us Maxi, but we managed to stay up! We didn't get the drop thanks to an unexpected victory by NK Medjimurje in a match against our direct rivals for relegation. We certainly wouldn't have succeeded if Miroslav and I hadn't taken part in that seminar. During a crisis period when our coach was up to his neck in deep water, we didn't lose our heads and didn't give in to attacks of despair. There's always a solution and the most important thing is maintaining a positive approach.

45. When you stop pedalling, you fall

The basis for successful performance in any job is a narrow specialisation, which is only possible if you've got the specific expertise. Expert knowledge can't be gained over a short period, by attending a course or by obtaining a certain football qualification. The process of development of coaching expertise is ongoing, it can last a lifetime. Coaches who don't supplement their basic knowledge on a daily basis usually fade away, leaving the stadium with their heads down and disappear into the greyness of mediocrity. The education of football coaches can be compared to cycling, Maxi. The moment you stop pedalling, you fall. The moment you stop educating and investing in yourself, you disappear from the coaching scene. If you're not constantly mastering new skills and knowledge, you'll be overtaken by your younger colleagues, who'll be eager to jump into your place. The worst is when your work becomes routine, and your knowledge deteriorates. So keep renewing your knowledge continually, Maxi. Study the literature, follow new trends, analyse the work of your successful colleagues. You could occasionally take part in a seminar to upgrade both your personal and technical skills. Don't just follow sport. You should also follow other aspects of society and expand your horizons. You'll always find certain benefits in each area that can be applied to your coaching job. You wouldn't believe how much I've absorbed from motivational videos on YouTube from other sports. I don't doubt you, Maxi. I know you won't let yourself fall behind. You're only at the beginning and there are a lot of unfulfilled goals in front of you.

46. Achieving prosperity helps the players

How many times have you been in a situation to help a fallen player but didn't do it, Maxi? You thought the trouble would pass and time would heal the wounds. Today, you surely regret you missed the opportunity to help him, or at least hug him. For me, as I went through various temptations from pills to living within the hell of alcohol addiction, then living in the Cenacolo Community for drug addicts, the most important thing I learned is that by helping others, I help myself the most. Players don't adore me for no reason, saying they've never had a better kit man in the club's history. This is because I always help them. I constantly have time for them always joking and smiling.

As I help them, in turn they help me. Helping is infectious. It's the experience and talent of every person in every situation. I always wonder why coaches and players don't help each other more. Each one of them is always on the go, rushing somewhere, forgetting to stop, talk and wait patiently. What a strange time we're living in! We've learned how to get rich, but we haven't learnt how to live. Our soul has been taken away by computers! We've ceased to communicate face-to-face. We want to gain respect and become successful overnight. Our communication has been reduced to email, facebook or twitter.

It seems I can't keep up with the times, Maxi. I keep wondering where on earth have human values disappeared to. If you want to build positive and friendly relationships with people Maxi, it's important to understand the purpose of support. Helping is not a waste of time! The moment you devote your time to a player, it's by no means a waste of time, but rather a great asset to you and the player. If you give a player the support, which may even be symbolic, a quick smile, a pat on the shoulder, or a hug, you're helping him to enhance an aspect of his life. When helping a player you're sending a message, expressing a positive attitude, understanding and caring about your player. Your message won't be left unnoticed. It also affects the other players, who'll copy you and start behaving in a similar way. The start of a positive atmosphere in the dressing room can be easily sparked with just one small gesture. Do you know how essential positive vibes in the dressing room are for you as a coach, Maxi? Priceless! Players are often lost within the fog of the outside world which knows no warm words, where helping words are unknown. Life which players face outside the stadium is on the one hand, focused on the fight for a harsh existence and on the other, making and spending money. As a coach you're able to spread kindness with a positive attitude and help others, but you also can spoil the mood of everyone around you with your miserable sourness. In your smile I can see you've understood the point – we shape our own attitude and we're able to manage it. Within the choice, you should choose a positive attitude. Help others and yourself and you'll be constantly happy.

47. Players follow a coach out of respect or fear

In order to be followed obediently, admired and respected by your players, Maxi, you have to impose yourself as an authority. When appointed as a coach you became the formal authority, an authority by function. This authority is only temporarily accepted by the players. Over time, if you're not accepted by the players, your formal authority, given your function, will be ignored in a short space of time. Authority, unlimited power, is not given to you 'carte blanche' - actual authority has to be acquired through your personality, expertise, work, performance and honesty. Players are extremely smart, so you shouldn't ever underestimate them. They quickly assess and judge what kind of person you are. Are you someone credible, consistent, correct, fair or honest? Only with truly built authority and trust, can respect of the players be gained. Players are wise and they differentiate between 'coaches with authority', who are valued and respected, and 'coaches who have power', who are not. A coach with authority is followed out of respect, and the 'powerful' coach is obeyed out of fear. To respect and follow you, Maxi, you have to be able to solve their problems and potential conflicts that always might be experienced in some form in the team. Players expect you to be a good teacher of the game, someone who'll educate and inspire them.

The better you meet their expectations, the stronger your value will be in their eyes. The authority that is based on partnership and mutual respect between coach and player is long term. The key values of a coach in building this partnership with his players are fairness and honesty.

48. Should players like the coach?

In terms of a coach's role it's irrelevant whether the players like him or not. It's important that the coach adopts the correct attitude towards players. Successful coaches have the highest regard for fairness, integrity and achievement of common goals. On many occasions I've heard how various 'do-gooders' tried to persuade the coach to make a move at the expense of others which would increase his popularity and success. A coach should never allow himself to be persuaded to do this. The main criteria for doing certain things should always be its level of correctness and not a goal that can be achieved, regardless of increasing popularity or achieving sports success. Coaches who stick to these guidelines are respected by players and remain long in this ungrateful role. Therefore, in communication with your players, Maxi, you have to adopt an attitude of truth and justice, because this is highly valued and respected among players. There'll always be those on the team who simply see themselves as 'football stars' and due to their football talent they're above you and the other players. They even dare to criticise you and raise their voice in public. In such cases, you mustn't succumb to external pressures. A correct and honest approach to all your players and the public will secure your inner peace and allow a smooth operation without paying attention to this type of criticism. It feels good when players are influenced by their coach's procedures which are in line with his words and his behaviour. Successful coaches are unanimous in their attitude - the greatest success in sport is easiest to achieve with those who are modest and humble. Would Luka Modric, one of Real Madrid's flagship players, ever have unlocked his greatness if he hadn't been modest and humble in failure as well as in success?

49. The captain understands the game and the coach's ideas

Maxi, I'll tell you why a successful coach always insists that the captain should be his choice. The team captain is the coach's right-hand man on the pitch. It's understandable that the captain can only be a person who enjoys the coach's unlimited trust. Equally, the captain needs to really understand the game and the coach's ideas. During the selection process, there mustn't be a false democracy and players must fully accept the coach's decision. It's crucial that the player has authority among the players, is a first team regular with a moral character. He also has to understand the game and know how to communicate. When selecting a captain, coaches are very demanding. They have to be, since the captaincy role is an essential link in the success of the team. The captain must lead his teammates in training and on match day. The captain has to know how the team is organized and its way of playing. Furthermore, the captain is the person who informs the coach about problems brewing in the team. The captain needs to assess which issues should be passed on to the coach, and he should know which challenges can be solved with a physical therapist or by the coach's assistants. The captaincy role among young players is priceless. The influence of the captain in developing the minds of young players can often be more useful than that of the actual coach. Only the captain can persuade young players that sacrifice is part and parcel of professional sport and without it there's no success. The coach should never set unrealistic objectives for the captain and players. If a coach's assessment suggests the team should reach seventh or eighth place, he should never force the captain and players to believe they could reach first or second place. At best, the coach must ignite the team's hope that eventually, at maximum effort and unity, they could fight for third or fourth place, which would lead to an international competition. The captain and the players may also assess the realistic possibilities of their own team - although some coaches tend not to think so.

50. Team success without prima donnas

For any coach, the team selection is a complex and responsible task – something you'd know well yourself, Maxi. The coach should never choose players who hold the exact same qualities as one another. The coach should choose players who are best suited to a particular position. The ideal choice for a coach is a combination of football experts and uncompromising fighters; players with a strong character and athletic personalities. Naturally, it can't be the same to create a team in Croatia, where players have enviable technical and tactical knowledge, as here in Ireland, where players' technical skills aren't so obvious. However, certain other qualities are more expressed, such as agility, speed, and a fighting spirit. I agree with your statement Maxi that mastery of the ball is no longer enough to fight among the serious leagues. The complete player should possess technical and tactical knowledge along with a formed character, confidence, athletic qualities, work ethic, team mentality and, above all, a healthy lifestyle. The coach needs to explain to each player what his specific role in the team is and what's expected from him in order to be ready for all the challenges he faces during the season. Each player must be aware that the tasks given to him need to be achieved. If there's no one in the team who behaves like a prima donna, the team is destined for great success. If, however, there's such an individual in the team who only plays for himself, you can hardly expect a better result. Players who act in this way strive for self-promotion with their performance and attitude. The biggest problem for a coach with a prima donna attitude occurs when he doesn't do his job at the moment when the ball is lost. These kinds of players directly threaten the result of the team. In turn, his work has to be done by another player, which requires extra effort. Another problem for a coach with this type of player in his squad is the player's skills and creative lucidity, which often gains the sympathy of the public and the media. Unfortunately, Maxi, you too have a prima donna in the team, who loves self-promotion and does things his own way. In my modest opinion, his behaviour was the cause of our last defeat at Oriel Park. He's a young, talented player and it would be a shame to drop him. The only option you've got is to talk to him in depth Maxi, and try to explain with a lot of empathy and understanding that what he's doing is harming himself and equally the team. You should constantly encourage him to change his approach to the game, motivate him to understand that playing for a team, actually means playing for yourself. Converting an individual to a team-player may take time and be bumpy along the way, but it's surely worth the effort as these individuals are, more or less, excellent football talents and our

Richie is that for sure. The worst option is to leave him out of the team, as this leads to confrontation with the public and also the media which is the last thing I want to happen to you.

51. Players need to know what is expected of them

Every player should always know what's expected of him and what he can gain from the coach and his assistants. Meeting for the first time, the coach needs to explain to the players that the common goal of the team is always ahead of individual interest. Maxi, how do you prepare your players before a game? Most coaches motivate players by giving them a speech, yet equally, there are plenty of coaches who tend to provide an overview of expectations and detailed information about the next opponent in writing. I prefer coaches who give a short, stimulating and encouraging speech before a match. In my opinion, a dull piece of paper, no matter how much relevant information it contains, can't replace the personal contact and emotion that coaches convey to their players. I say this as primarily the coach has plenty of time during week-long preparations before the match to inform players about important details relating to the game and the opponent. I like the philosophy of the wise Chinese Sun in which commanders of the army, and that's exactly what you coaches are, should always aim to beat the opponent before the match begins. In order to succeed you need studious preparation, good knowledge of your opponent and a lot of tactical exercises and meetings with your players. The entire week before the game, coaches have to work on the preparation and motivation of the players for the upcoming match. Based on this, the players should know the prepared strategy on the day of the match by heart and would be ready for every possible situation and surprise. After preparations for the match are complete, every other form of motivation, apart from a brief speech on the eve of the match would seem counter-productive and would probably make players feel tense. During preparations, a successful coach never humiliates his rivals or their coaches and players. He equally treats his players in the same way. In addition to the team as a whole, during the week he endeavours to motivate each individual player. Young players shouldn't need to be particularly motivated as they are really eager to prove themselves and anxious to take advantage of the opportunity.

52. Notice your players and see the rewards

During the competitive season, coaches are usually more concerned with how players perform their tactical tasks than the team results. I think you too, Maxi, are constantly focusing on how to get the best out of your players. To be able to do that, you need a sense of peace and harmony in the team. Every time you have the opportunity, try to isolate yourself from external influences. Players know how to relax, especially the younger ones, so they constantly need to be encouraged and motivated to work hard. They need to be motivated to follow their instructions as this leads to the perfection of performance to achieve the desired game. To be able to do that, you have to get each player to understand that he plays an important role in achieving the common goal. Lots of conversations, praise and a positive approach always create good results. When the players are convinced that you notice them, that you appreciate their hard work and dedication, they'll give their best in training and matches. Players shouldn't only be encouraged to develop their football skills. At least once a week you should work with them on developing their emotional and social skills. When I was a coach in Croatia, my key player, a midfielder, used to be distracted at every home match by the abusive comments shouted from the crowds, which affected his play. I talked to him about it during each preparation, drawing his attention to focus only on the game and not to be distracted by the shouts from the fans. Before an important match, during my motivational speech for the game, I would hang a large picture of a cat chasing a mouse in the dressing room. I did this to explain to them that the cat doesn't think about whether someone is watching while hunting the mouse. The cat is completely focused on how to catch its prey - the little mouse. It reacts by instinct. That's a reaction I looked for from the players, to behave like cats in a game. I asked them to fully focus on the game to bring us victory and not the screaming comments from the crowd, or the wrong decisions of the referee. When I motivated them to behave like a cat, I actually asked my players to go through the match with a hunter's instinct. This went down really well with the players. That type of motivation, given through a story, proved to be very encouraging and built a positive team spirit. The higher the frequency of praise and encouragement on my part, the better the positive atmosphere in the team. I also noticed when it comes to younger players, that it's better to praise their performance immediately after an exercise than at a meeting after training. Compliments are very encouraging, but they must never be given without reason Maxi. They should be only given when truly deserved. The same for criticism. When players are ineffective in their performance, show understanding for this, but also point out the mistake and give them a solution for it. All players have their bad days and they'll appreciate it when their coach shows understanding and not an immediate lesson because of a poor performance.

53. Players cannot be guided on the basis of praise alone

It's quite normal for experienced coaches to accept that players need to relax from time to time and the fact that sometimes they can get up to mischief. It's human and natural. Most young men, at some point during their youth, are unable to resist life's naughty temptations and go off the rails in their behaviour. There are usually two tactics successful coaches use when faced with behavioural issues from the players. One is used in mild circumstances. It consists of complete ignorance or disregard to the inappropriate behaviour of the player. Coaching practice has shown that this behaviour of the players, if simply ignored by the coach, eventually fades away and disappears. Another tactic is applied when the player's behaviour has put themselves or others at risk, or when they disturb the team activities and tarnish the reputation of the club. In this case, the coach should immediately react. In private, the player in question should be informed such behaviour will not be tolerated and must stop instantly, otherwise punishment will follow. This attitude should be consistent, which means that the coach is willing to drop such a player from the team or even club, regardless of his status and previous performance on the pitch. Maxi, penalising players should only be undertaken if that's what you're really forced to do. But once you've decided to go for it, it should be carried out properly and effectively. You have to accept it's impossible to lead the players only on the basis of praise or expectations and that inappropriate behaviour will simply disappear by itself. I once knew a coach who used to punish his player's behaviour by getting them to sing in a public place chosen by the coach. As a young coach he was ambitious and would financially penalise players for each offence. After some time he realised that he was always trying to punish the behaviour of the same player and that he wasn't using the same disciplinary measures for the entire team. In contrast, the singing punishment proved to be very effective. This was confirmed by one of his players who had to sing in front of two hundred guests during pre-season training in Spain.

54. Respect your players

Maxi, do you drive a BMW? I ask this because today coaches are often evaluated through the prism of their material achievement. Even the car they drive could be a means of assessing their performance. Qualities such as expertise, sports results, honesty, wisdom, and respect are often neglected. I wonder Maxi, where did the basic human values that we were raised on and taught by our parents disappear? Respect has gone. Are China, America and Japan the only places on earth left where the coach or teacher is actually respected? Despite all of this, I don't want to believe that the reality is so dark and gloomy.

The most effective way of gaining respect in the coaching profession is when the coach himself shows interest and a positive attitude towards players and co-workers, towards their feelings, attitudes and habits. A successful coach respects his players, colleagues and co-workers, takes care of them and encourages them to progress. How many times have we tried to stop somebody talking because we didn't agree with them? How many times have we criticised players for a 'wrong' move? How often have we shared advice even without being asked? Respect players Maxi, always make the first move to solve a dispute, let journalists freely express their opinions, praise the environment in which you perform and you'll be a successful coach. The role of a coach is becoming increasingly demanding day by day. Coaches are constantly expected to do more and better themselves. One doesn't have to be too wise to notice that mutual respect within the team develops a general respect for the club, including the management, sponsors and officials. The way players treat you, Maxi, their attitude towards the club and training - with respect, or lack of it, depends on how much respect they previously developed growing up at home. It also certainly depends on the amount of respect you're willing to show them as a coach. Every coach should be aware of this and so should you. It's immensely important that coaches accept the share of responsibility in how players behave. As a role model, the coach certainly affects the way his players behave. Does their behaviour fit into the communication etiquette of the civilised club? There are so many more elements, along with respect that are necessary and important to be a successful coach.

The coach himself is the one who should be able to recognise the importance of all elements affecting his coaching success. Teaching sports skills requires broad expertise which has to be continually supplemented with additional education. Players always expect positive impetus from the coach.

Players are the ones who use the coaches' expertise and experience to realize their sporting goals. The opinion of the coach is often a critical stance for most players. Players need respect from the coach and his support. I don't know a single case where a player succeeded without the support of a coach and if there is one, it's a rare thing. Not a single player will succeed without a good teacher. If the coach doesn't respect the players, players won't respect him either. If the coach has a negative attitude about everything, everyone around him will become a loser. Good always attracts good, Maxi.

55. How to 'strip down' the players

Have you ever been taught statistics in school, Maxi? I was taught in school that statistics is an element of applied mathematics that deals with the collection, processing, interpretation and presentation of data. Statistics wasn't exactly my favourite subject at school and I never would have imagined my friends as football coaches would use them with so much enthusiasm. Statistics become a critical tool for coaches in making crucial decisions. Thanks to statistics, coaches know how far players run, how many passes they make, and how many of them are complete or incomplete. Just as a high jumper knows the exact height he jumped, coaches also have very precisely measured indicators of player performance.

Today, thanks to the sophisticated tracking system, using cameras installed at the stadium, it's possible to gain extremely useful data that provides your professional team real insight into the physical and technical possibilities of individual players and the entire team. With the results that can be obtained, coaches today can completely 'strip down' footballers to basic statistical analysis – metres run, fouls made, accuracy of passes etc. Statistics help the coach and club management, but also journalists, to be more objective in giving an assessment of somebody's performance. Without these exact indicators it certainly wouldn't be possible. The great thing about the power of statistics is that everyone who doesn't understand the game of football, can understand statistical indicators pretty well. Regardless of the exact indicators obtained, the overall performance of players during a game is immeasurable as the statistical indicators are used more to 'strip down' the players.

56. Accelerate the recovery of players

Maxi, can you imagine my expert team without our doctor Samir? Today, without working with a medical expert, it's practically impossible to achieve good results. Although the most common public perception is that the primary role of the physician is to treat and rehabilitate athletes, this is only partly true. In addition to the ongoing concern of the treatment and rehabilitation of athletes, he plays an essential role in the field of nutrition and monitoring the training process. The physician himself, without cooperation from the coach, simply wouldn't be able to protect athletes from injuries. Cooperation from the coach is essential, as it's important a coach has at least a basic understanding of sports medicine and recognises the scope of a doctor's work in the team. Muscle analysis is crucial in preventing athletes from getting injured. Players who trained with me, knew in advance that at the beginning of each season certain measurements of muscle strength were to be achieved. After experts performed detailed analysis of muscle groups of each player and later on through the training process, any deficiencies identified during testing were corrected through individual work. Cooperation with the doctor proves to be essential in assessing the ability of an injured athlete. As coaches try to accelerate the recovery of athletes and their return to the pitch, doctors are always sceptical, convinced returning is premature.

Maxi, I noticed regardless of how much the injured player is essential to the team, you always hand the final decision to our doctor and his ethics which oblige him not to allow an insufficiently recovered player back on the pitch. Although, I must say there have been cases, before you arrived at the club, when the former club doctor accepted the risk, at the cost of re-injury.

Coaches and doctors must also cooperate in the fight against the use of banned substances through continuous education and the constant philosophy that these drugs are detrimental to their health. Maxi, you'll probably agree with me, sports success can never be more important than human health.

57. Right food leads to high performance

Strandfield House is my favourite when it comes to healthy food. I just love their green soup. When did you last eat at Strandfield House, Maxi? A healthy diet is extremely important for the players, because it helps optimal development, good concentration and increases durability and resistance. Science has proved that the basic processes of releasing energy needed for intense physical effort are directly related to the quantity and quality of a player's diet. The daily balanced diet of players should be rich in vitamins, minerals and other nutritional substances. In sports nutrition, an adequate intake of proteins that build muscles and carbohydrates filling the energy reserve readily available in the body is extremely important. The consumption of vitamins and minerals is increased for players. These must be taken in the form of rich foods or supplements. Footballers should eat as much fresh, natural food as they can find. Thanks to spending time with players for many years I've noticed that players who eat proper foods can maintain a high training intensity, recover faster from injuries and achieve better results. When we talk about the importance of nutrition for the players, the importance of water intake is often neglected. Water is particularly important for a player's body. Players consume large quantities during training and matches. The body needs to compensate for the fluids lost through sweating because even low dehydration of 2% can significantly reduce the effect of a player in a game. Regarding the most suitable diet for a player, coaches should consult a doctor and a nutritionist. The operational process of ordering and controlling the food for the players in restaurants should be left to the club's physiotherapist. In addition to the recommendations of doctors and nutritionists, in relation to the right diet, coaches can also rely on their own experience or the experience of those he trusts. An interesting example is a personal approach to diet by Croatian coach Zlatko Ivankovic, who insists on a large consumption of honey in his players' diets. When I discussed this with him, I learned that he insists on the highest possible consumption of honey due to the high content of vitamins and minerals. The content of protein, amino acids and enzymes gives honey added value because this is great for cell regeneration after intensive training. Along with this, honey is rich in essential amino acids that the human body can't produce, so it must be taken with food.

58. Let's give the players what they want

There's only one way to motivate players, Maxi. The only way you can influence players to assure maximum commitment to football and the training sessions is to give them what they want. And what exactly do they want? Almost every player wants to achieve a successful playing career, to play for a big club, and to be important and appreciated. Every player wants to express his creativity and personality to the maximum. Tell me Maxi, which one of our players is thinking about their health, family and the future? All of them first of all want to be recognized and respected in their environment. A coach who manages to deepen the sense of personal importance in a player will turn him into a friend and those who don't comply usually face difficulties in communication with other players. Try, therefore, to deepen the sense of personal importance in each of your players. It's nothing new or unknown. Feeling recognised and respected is one of the most important needs of every human being. Every player craves for the approval of those who they're in contact with. They all want their efforts and their true value recognised among those who follow sport. Every player genuinely cares about recognition from the public. How can you persuade players to give maximum effort during training and on the pitch?

Only when you manage to create a good relationship with the players and a strong spirit among the players, will you be able to ignite their enthusiasm and inspire what's most valuable to them. Experience has taught me that there's nothing as disastrous for the player's will and ego as criticism from the coach. Criticising and belittling the players is not effective. Far more can be achieved by showing encouragement and sharing praise.

Genuine praise is the recipe for successful communication with your players. In giving praise and credit to players, a coach can always show his honesty. I know certain coaches who have a habit of flattering players. Flattery rarely achieves anything with players as they can spot exactly what's genuine and what isn't. Mere flattery is doomed to fail, although unfortunately there are some players who crave for recognition and enjoy it even if they don't deserve it. This also applies to certain coaches, Maxi - "Don't be afraid of the enemy who attacks you, but rather the friend who flatters you".

59. Players are the best customers

The Chinese have a saying which Croatian coaches working in China have positively taken on board. It says "the one who does not smile should not play a merchant's role". I'll tell you a story about this Maxi, told to me by Croatian coach Drazen Besek. It was the first lesson he mastered in China. One Wednesday, he received a call from his agent who told him that on Saturday he should be in Shanghai as the Chinese Premier League club Shanghai Shenhua was interested in him as a coach. He was surprised that a club as far away as China had shown interest in him, yet for someone who's always ready for a challenge, it didn't take long for him to decide to go. As always, he tried to make a positive impression in negotiations for the job. During the ten-hour long flight he made the effort to read everything he possibly could about China, its history and culture. When he finally arrived in Shanghai, the club's president was there waiting for him at the airport. He was given a very warm welcome. With a constant smile on the president's face, he spoke to Drazen in a very friendly and fluid manner. He knew everything about him, his coaching career and his success with NK Varteks in the Cup Winners' Cup in 1998. Although he knew the Chinese are a very polite nation, he certainly didn't expect so much warmth at the first meeting.

After dinner, around midnight, while saying goodbye, the president approached him again and shared an additional couple of compliments on his account, praising him as a pleasant conversationalist. Delighted with the way things turned out, the Croatian coach returned to his hotel feeling good.

While lying in bed before going to sleep, trying to make sense of the impressions from dinner, he realised he wasn't a good merchant after all. Why? He came to China intending to sell himself as a well-known and renowned Croatian coach and to do so at a certain price. What actually happened was that he was bought by them. What can we conclude from this story, Maxi? Being friendly, smiling, knowing people's names and certain aspects of somebody's life can disarm anyone – just like my friend, the famous Croatian coach. He actually became the coach of Shanghai Shenhua for a lesser amount of money than what he'd planned. He didn't regret it as his Chinese friends taught him that warmth and a friendly smile are the best goods to sell. The players of Croatian Premier League club Osijek, know this very well as today they're coach Drazen Besek's number one recipients of his compliments – the right words open every door, Maxi. What goes around, comes around.

60. How to get players to listen to your advice

Many coaches make mistakes as they want players to buy into their views at all costs. No one likes to listen to advice and instructions, not even the players. We would all prefer to work according to our conscience and feel that our decisions are respected and praised. Players prefer when coaches respect them as a person, when they're asked about their hopes and when their work and effort is respected. As I often say to you, Maxi, during my visit to Croatia I spent a lot of time talking with Croatian football coaches. In addition to talking about topics the two of us are talking about right now, we would often go back in time remembering our former coaches and their styles of training. We remembered one particular late Croatian coach, who coached us when we were just young lads. He was a gentleman and a great pedagogue, who never gave direct commands. He would never have say to players "do this and that!" or "don't do this and that"! The 'instructions' from our favourite coach were always given in the form of advice and suggestions such as "I suggest you do this", "maybe you could try it another way"! Only today, and that's a good thirty years later, can I realistically perceive the quality and greatness of his communication. With such a distinctive way of communication he was building our self-criticism as young players and encouraging us to train hard and cooperate with others. It's an interesting question to ask why today's modern coaches don't act in the same way.

61. Is victory the peak of a coaching job?

For sports fans and the public, victory often represents the peak, but for me, being on the inside of the club, victory represents more about the current delight of fans than an indicator of the success of a coach. To me, creating a game plan for the team, creating a positive atmosphere in and around the club, ensuring fan satisfaction with something to look forward to, represents the greatest achievement of a coach. The game plan is a system that the coach uses to develop his own style of play, in order to achieve success. This game plan is the implementation of the style of play that a coach has already mapped out. Successfully putting the game plan of the team into practice on the pitch, regardless of the occasional defeat, brings coaches inner peace and serenity, and successful results for the club. Success is a powerful weapon in the process of building a team, because it gives credibility to coaches and serves as a motivation to players for further work and progress. So, I see the process of creating the game, creating top players and nurturing a positive atmosphere as the highlights of a coaching position, Maxi. Certainly, creating a game plan is not an easy job at all. Faith in yourself, knowledge and perseverance always bring results. I would be foolish to say that victory over rivals shown in the results isn't important. It is and always will be important because it ensures survival for a coach. Having said that, a successful coach takes victory personally only as a tool he needs to create the outside appearances of his success and his club's success. The public doesn't share this opinion. The sports public experiences a coach's success on the basis of his results alone. A good result can be deceptive, and can often pacify the coach. Victories breed complacency, and strengthen the ego of a coach. Glory is the worst disease that can affect a player or a coach. Many, after winning a trophy, simply get carried away, forgetting their roots, their friends, and their first club. My Croatian friends, coaches of worldwide reputation, and your successful Irish colleagues, are no different from other coaches. I know this from personal experience. We're all made of flesh and blood. All of you are going to succumb to the euphoria of the outer appearances. The magnificent success of qualifying for the World Cup with the national team of Iran, equally absorbed my friend, at that point the already experienced coach Branko Ivankovic; celebrated in the media, invited to a host of events, and even the President's guest in a country of 80 million residents. How can you resist the overwhelming bandwagon of success? Luckily, my friend quickly kept his two feet firmly on the ground away from the media intoxication created by an external impression. Thanks to learning from his mistakes and continuous development, he quickly realized that glory is temporary and he now prefers to enjoy the good harmony of the players, friends and family than the victory that had brought him fame. High quality communication with the players and the public brought him safety, strengthened his coaching position, and eliminated the fear of failure. Gaining inner peace is not easy to reach. A successful coach tries to find inner peace through humility and dedication to the players, fans and the media. Why is inner peace so important? Inner peace opens the door to success for the coach, giving him the strength to persevere in the creation of the game, in the playing progress of the club and the squad he coaches. Let me assure you Maxi, when you find your creative peace, when you get to reach the desired game plan although you're still creating it now Maxi, you'll win championships, cups, and attract crowds to the stadiums! If you fail to create a game, you'll start to slide toward mediocrity, and this is anything but success.

62. A successful coach embraces his own weaknesses

Life's rapid pace and the daily struggle to achieve objectives don't leave much time for coaches themselves and their personal development. Despite this, every coach should find time to devote to himself. Every coach should look internally at himself as much as possible. Success in life depends not so much on how hard you work, but on how well you think. Respecting yourself and others, being self-critical, listening to others, and understanding and admitting your mistakes are requirements that a man needs to meet at the very start in order to become a fulfilled and mature person. Have you, Maxi, made efforts to live a peaceful, fulfilled and happy life?

Only spiritual development can truly bring people joy and happiness. Spiritual development builds a positive attitude not only within yourself, but also to the surrounding environment. A happy and fulfilled man can only become one who is ready to embrace his weaknesses, the one who learns from his mistakes and the one who recognises his qualities and uses them to his advantage. Great is the one who, in addition to admitting them, has the courage to resolve his own problems. Such people are happy and successful, as their mental state and perspectives don't depend on others.

63. In life no effort is wasted

"What are the most important qualities needed to achieve coaching success?". You're not the only one who has asked me this question, Maxi. This is what all young coaches ask. Although they all, considering my age and experience, expect some sort of great wisdom from me, I'll probably disappoint them with a simple and humble answer: an immense love for people and for football, many painstaking hours of hard work and perseverance. In this I always emphasise that no effort in life is in vain. Every effort, however, even the smallest, is always worth it, and it's always fertilised in some form, either materially or spiritually. If a man loves something enthusiastically, if you give your all and trust everything inside of you to become something good and positive - nothing will prevent you from achieving your set goal. The truth is, there'll always be thorns and roses along the way to the finish line, but it's fully worth the effort and worth a try. Be persistent, constantly absorb new knowledge and develop yourself, because this is the only way to reach the results you want. Young coaches are impatient and often find it a challenge to work as an assistant, with ideas of immediately becoming a head coach. Young coaches should be taught from the very beginning of their coaching career that this is a big mistake which they'll only realise later in their profession. Sometimes a young coach can be faced with a great opportunity and can even experience a sudden success, but without the necessary experience this success can quickly turn from a 'flash-in-the-pan' to the bubble being burst. And then the journey from then on can be very difficult and painful, and often impossible. The road to coaching success is not an overnight journey from victory to defeat, it's a long-term process – it's a marathon, not a sprint. It's a route with many stops along the way and with constant checks. These constant evaluation points are the best motivation boosters to achieve continuous future success measured by results. Coaches are constantly put in risky situations accepting a variety of challenges. The challenges force them to constantly invest in themselves, either through additional professional education, or through working on themselves in order to strengthen self-control and concentration. Coaches are actually eternally addicted to objectives and challenges. You're not alone, as all of us working in sports are like that. I simply can't imagine life without goals or challenges. Challenges are by far my best fix, filling me with adrenaline, forcing me to give my best and grab them with both hands.

64. The difficulties in achieving a successful coaching career

Maxi, you asked me why so many former players, who were successful in their playing careers, had not achieved similar success as a coach. A successful coaching career is difficult to achieve because of the many characteristics coaches need to have. It's merely not enough to possess the basic elements that all former great players undoubtedly have, such as football knowledge and experience. Other characteristics and skills of the individual are crucial, namely intelligence, character, effective communication and attitude. There's also courage, responsibility, self-control, a teamwork ethic and hard work. As you know, I also had a previous career as a great player, and that started me off with a great advantage. The charisma I had as a top player was the key that opened the door to every club, but to my regret that same key didn't unlock the door to my coaching greatness. My glorious playing career and coaching talent were not enough to control my various personal issues, such as arriving drunk at the training sessions. If you take a closer look, you can easily discover the majority of former top players who had successful playing careers, fail over time as a coach, with honourable exceptions such as Jupp Heynckes and Carlo Ancelotti. The best example of this is Maradona, one of the best players in the history of football.

The majority of former top players are convinced that the mere fact that they were top football players is enough to position them at the very top in the coaching profession. Only hard-working, persevering coaches with human virtues, fully dedicated to the team on a daily basis, can achieve a successful coaching career. Believe me, a coach can't be successful if he has a vice, such as gambling, betting or alcohol, as I had.

65. What does success mean?

Each of us wants to be successful in the job we do. Since the beginning of mankind, man has been constantly striving for something better, more beautiful and more perfect. The same applies to you, Maxi, as a sports coach. Coaches are constantly striving for something better and bigger. Whether it's about the players, results, clubs or money, they always strive for more. Since I started to work as a kit man in our club, I've seen a dozen senior team coaches come and go. The most successful were those who, apart from knowing their job, were aware that the key to success is in themselves. What we are depends on what we think. Each investment in the fundamental principles of success, honesty and perseverance, will always be more than repaid. In an effort to create a high-quality relationship with the players, management and the media, successful coaches can often change their attitudes and way of working. If we're not willing to change, it's highly possible we've reached our maximum potential. For years I've watched many of your successful predecessors Maxi, changing their attitude and behaviour during their stay at the club in order to get the maximum from the players, compared with others who have insisted on the players changing themselves in order to adapt to them. No change is easy, but with strong faith, a great desire and perseverance anything can be achieved. I see you're worried because you lost the last game at Oriel Park, Maxi. You don't have to worry about defeat, as victory and defeat are an integral part of the coaching job. Moreover, defeat doesn't even have to be a mistake, it can sometimes be the best thing to happen to a coach at just the right time. You have to learn to accept defeat but only temporarily. "Failures are the steps to success" - someone once beautifully said. There's not one coach who hasn't faced painful defeats and failures at the beginning of his career. It takes time until they realise failure is just part of the lessons that lead them to success. Your last defeat, although it may seem at this point so painful, isn't your first, and believe me - it won't be your last.

You say that you were afraid of this match? Would the football team of my small, recently established Croatia have ever won third place at the World Cup at France 98 if the coach Miroslav Blazevic, was afraid of failure? Failure is an integral part of the pathway in life that everybody must walk along. The more spiritual and more persistent we become, the less failure and more success to follow there will be. If you consider your coaching role as a reflection of fulfilment, respect, focus and an immense love for the sport, you'll achieve success in your coaching career, regardless of the results.

66. I've always stood up for what burns inside me

Most of the public who follow sport consider coaches as very sociable people. People who are never alone, always surrounded by others. Is this just an illusion or is this the reality, Maxi? You as a coach for sure know that this is a mere illusion. Interestingly, the role of a coach is actually quite lonely. Coaches are mostly self-denying people who always open new roads, perceive new opportunities when others fail to notice them and enjoy being alone deep within their thoughts. They're always thinking two steps ahead. And because of this they're often misunderstood and criticized. How to resist it? We shouldn't resist. We just have to be ourselves. The coach needs to tap into all of the resources and means he can think of to impose his attitude. A successful coach won't accept nor support anything that seems mediocre. A successful coach always stands up for what burns inside of him. With all due respect, every coach should listen to other people's opinions and advice, but accept and take on board only what contributes to his vision of excellence. The game of football not only requires the good physical condition of players, but also the willingness of their heart and mind. Sometimes players are in excellent physical shape, but their 'heart' is far from ready. Have you ever found yourself in a situation when your mind wants to take control of your body, but the body refuses to cooperate? In football it's the same as in life. All 'family members' - the body, mind and heart have to work together. The game will never be complete if even only one member, either body, mind or heart, doesn't participate in the game.

67. The philosophy of coaching as part of the family

They say behind every successful man there's a woman, and vice versa. Also, behind every successful coach there's his coaching philosophy. This term refers to how coaches perceive players and in turn create relationships with them. After so many years of friendship and spending time with coaches I noticed that all of them perceive the philosophy of the coaching experience as if it's an integral part of their family. This doesn't surprise me, as they've shaped, built and grown with it, the same way as they've built their family over the years. And you Maxi have also incorporated much of your own temperament and character into your coaching philosophy. There's no successful philosophy or superior results without enthusiasm and passion. Each coaching philosophy has its own distinctive handwriting. Coaching philosophy isn't created, as some people simplify it, from game to game or from victory to defeat. It's built and matured over many years. The creation of your coaching philosophy Maxi, is influenced by your education, your family and the environment in which you were raised. It also consists of a great deal of published words and generally accepted beliefs that you've read in books or heard on television, building up over the years into a library or database in your head. As someone who's familiar with the coaching style of my friends, Branko Ivankovic and Drazen Besek, Croatian coaches who have worked in China, I recognise the great impact of China's spiritual way of thinking in their coaching philosophy. Initially, I recognised the ideology they adopted from the great Chinese teacher Sun Tzu, author of one of the world's best-selling books "The Art of War". Sun Tzu's thoughts aren't what the book's title might suggest, only applicable to the military aspects of human activity. The fundamental philosophical ideas from the book, such as victory over the enemy before the fight, my coaching friends now apply to their coaching. Their philosophy of coaching equals their perspective on life which has been shaped over time. It's a guideline which determines the methods of their work, their relationships with the players and how to form a game. Maxi, you really should read this book. Believe me, you won't regret it. As a young coach building your own coaching philosophy, you mustn't forget to include your personality in forming your own philosophy of coaching, regardless of the fact that your coaching role and your behaviour will be considerably influenced by your set goals.

68. Think positively and see how your life changes

Maxi, have you noticed that there are lots of coaches who constantly have something to complain about? They complain about the referees and officials, the players, the management, the media, or low wages. For so many coaches, moaning and regret is a common characteristic and even after a string of sporting successes or a strong financial deal, they simply can't hide their dissatisfaction. Surely, this isn't healthy. The constant gloom does nothing but enhance the negativity even further, creating a vicious circle. There isn't one coach who has ever strengthened his position by complaining about the players, referees, management, fans or the media. Contrary to the plan, this would only inflame the anger making things worse. I once knew a coach who would forever blame the referee for the defeat. Not only did he fail to gain anything from his negative comments, the only thing he did manage to ever gain was damage. His referee complaints provoked ridicule among the sporting public which interpreted his actions as a search for an excuse for his team's defeat. Having a negative approach to all aspects of coaching can do a lot of damage to the coaches as their attention diverts from the good things that are happening to them at work. A coach, who possesses an already embedded negative attitude, will hinder his own chances of happiness and enjoying the beautiful game. Maxi, I've certainly noticed you're not someone who constantly complains. In fact, I would say you switch things around, nurturing a positive attitude. Your view of the world around you is positive and I'm sure that a positive attitude and appreciation for this influences the quality of your life. In football there have and always will be situations where it's difficult to adopt a positive mind-set. What positives can be found in a situation where you've been severely betrayed by the referee, when he unfairly turns the game in favour of your rival? A positive attitude doesn't mean to mislead or ignore the facts, but regardless of the circumstances, we can again choose to be positive or negative. We make a choice. It's certainly easier to get into a negative frame of mind, than a positive one. How can we avoid a negative attitude? Just like most things in life, a positive attitude and gratitude can be learned by practice. 'Positive thinking' should be exercised. For me, the best exercise is when I'm in bed just before going to sleep. I go through the day in my mind and focus on the good things that have happened and number all the things I can be thankful for. There are certain days when I can't think of many good things but I always manage to find at least one good thing, a person that I like or something good that has happened to me and I think about it evoking the most beautiful memories and pictures. Every time I think about someone negatively, I immediately remind myself that this person must have at least 5 times more positive qualities - I just haven't noticed them. Since cultivating an attitude of gratitude and positivity, the quality of my life has improved. It really has. I feel happier and more complete.

69. The coaching profession of tomorrow

We've entered the second stage of the 21st century. Have you noticed some kind of step forward compared to the last century, Maxi? Mechanical technology has been replaced by digital advancement, forest paths by running tracks, and street football by FIFA computer games. Football has become big business, where the stakes, but equally the risks, are tremendous, especially at an elite level. The aim of a coaching career is no longer security, but more about a coach's personal growth.

The commercialisation of sport is reflected in the evolution of the role of a coach. Ex-UEFA technical director former Scotland manager Andy Roxburgh didn't say without reason that "the coach's jacket hangs on a shaky hanger". Today, when football is reported in the media, it becomes more and more about the focus on the personality of actors and this creates an image that the fate of the club and the players are the sole responsibility of the coach – which is certainly not true, Maxi. The players are the ones who score, break records and win matches. Their quality largely depends on the financial situation at the club, whether clubs invest in sports academies or can afford the luxury of bringing in expensive players from abroad. The coaches of tomorrow won't be protected from the realities of life consisting of the irrational and emotional convictions of the sporting public. With such continuous pressure coaches can only deal with this by permanently educating themselves and redistributing their former tasks to their associates. It's inevitable that there'll be a change in the ethnic structure of the players with whom the coaches work. In such circumstances, a successful career can be achieved only by an educated coach with developed communication skills, who'll know how to harmonise the diversity of the players in terms of education, habits and religion. It's certain this diversity will encourage coaches to enrich their knowledge in the fields of language, culture, religion and the various habits and ways of life that are brought along with the players from other countries and even continents.

With the increased promotion of football within society, coaches will no doubt face the significant influence of the rich and popular players and, given their importance, financial stability and media popularity, they'll be supported by the ownership structure of football clubs. The change will also be noticed in the increased demand for physical preparation and player exertion due to the increasing number of official matches.

It's just a matter of time before the players, thanks to various breathing techniques and rapid recovery, begin the second half as fully energised as they were at the start of the match. Luckily, technique and medicine still have no such impact on our minds, attitudes and reactions. Our thoughts and feelings can be affected only by ourselves. The art of thought management is still invisible and impenetrable for the world of science. Its forces are powerful and it's left to each of us to find them and get to know them. Once found, we also find a solution to all the problems that burden us.

70. Greatness is attainable

No more stories. No more tea with Yuri. Yuri has been gone for a long time now. He took his well-deserved retirement and now spends the summer months in his home country of Croatia, in Novi Vinodolski, a small town on the Adriatic coast. His winter days are spent in Ireland, in Dundalk, where his children and grandchildren live. He left quietly, in a modest and humble manner, probably not even knowing that the players, after he'd left, put up his picture among other great images that belong to the legends of the club.

The morning training session had just finished. After showering, I went along with the players to the TV room, where we watched the live draw for a forthcoming 3rd round of the Champions League in Nyon. I was overwhelmed with joy when I discovered the name of our future opponents. God has brought us together again. We were drawn against the club where Yuri started his football career, all those years ago. We're going to Varazdin in Croatia. I'm really looking forward to meeting him again after such a long time. I never told him that I recorded all of our conversations during our daily chats over a cup of tea. I've listened to them at least a hundred times so far, ruthlessly drawing on Yuri's rich wisdom, football knowledge and his life's experiences. While listening to a recording of a conversation, I was struck by one of his sentences: "Knowledge is not to keep to yourself but to share with others." So much so that I immediately knew his knowledge and experience had to be published to share among coaches all around the world. How come I hadn't thought of it before? It would be really selfish of me to keep his knowledge, wisdom and experience exclusively to myself.

Thanks to Yuri I reached my place of wisdom. Spiritual teacher Sri Chinmoy once said: "Yesterday I was smart, because I wanted to change the world. Today I am wise and therefore I am changing myself". Thanks to Yuri, only after I started to work on myself did my first significant results of coaching success came knocking, my first titles, winning championships and matches in European competitions. What does it mean to work on myself? The answer is very simple. Be yourself. Learn from your mistakes, listen, develop and change. Be grateful for what you have. Today I'm a happy man. I have my health, knowledge, wonderful family and the best job in the world. Now I want to show to coaches across the planet that greatness is truly attainable. My trigger to greatness was Yuri.

Let this book be yours!

Five wise tips from Yuri

1. Focus on the present

It's good and reasonable to learn from the mistakes of the past, but you shouldn't think too much about them. You should live and work in the present - it will bring a secure future.

2. Avoid working in an unsettled environment

The organisation, management and operations of sports clubs, regardless of their ranking, are no secret. This data can be easily found by every coach. Don't rush and don't accept offers from clubs that are disorganised, with leaders who promise a lot yet perform poorly. Be sure you're making the right choice as the dissatisfaction while working in such clubs will unconsciously affect your performance and work within the team.

3. Do not accept offers where results are expected overnight

If you're out of a coaching job, that doesn't mean you have to rush and accept the first offer that comes along. These rarely turn out as you'd like them to with painful consequences. Are you ready to tarnish your good reputation because of a seemingly 'attractive' offer?

4. Be fair

Lies and currying favour are common methods used by players and fellow coaches in order to gain favour with the head coach. Appreciate the truth, be fair, thank those who serve the truth, no matter how painful or difficult it might be.

5. Get rid of stress

The coaching profession is extremely susceptible to stress. How to get rid of it? Firstly, think positive and plan your coaching profession. Don't be embarrassed to ask your new employer to put the agreed terms on paper. This small, painstaking move (at the time) will certainly relieve you of possible future stress.

Printed in Great Britain
by Amazon

21888887R00096